A GENTLE GIANT

Myrtle Stewart's Poetry & Memoirs

W. MYRTLE STEWART
1917 – 2016

Edited by
Wilton R. Stewart, PhD & Marquetta R. Stewart-Brown, JD

Copyright © 2021 by Wilton R. Stewart & Marquetta R. Stewart-Brown. All Rights Reserved.

No part of this publication may be reproduced, stored in a retrieval system, or transmitted in any form or by any means, electronic, mechanical, photocopying, recording, scanning, or otherwise, except as permitted under Section 107 or 108 of the 1976 United States Copyright Act, without either the prior permission of Wilton R. Stewart, PhD or Marquetta R. Stewart-Brown, JD.

ISBN 978-0-578-98038-6

ISBN 978-0-578-98194-9 (eBook)

DEDICATION ON A LIFE WELL LIVED

This publication is dedicated to the descendants of the Edwards and Craig family clans. Their African-American roots can be traced back to the early 1800s in American history. A reflection on one's ancestral thoughts and roots, from whence they came, will serve as a guiding light and inspiration to a generation's future.

Captured in the written expressions of this book are the echoes of a journey taken in the earlier years of W. Myrtle Stewart's life. The illustrated words and extractions of her journaled memoirs and poems were compiled and interwoven together by her son and daughter, Wilton R. Stewart, Ph.D. and Marquetta R. Stewart-Brown, JD. This publication serves as a tribute to Myrtle's love of writing poetry and phrases of wisdom. She was always prepared to offer an impromptu message and loved being asked to cite a poem or give an inspirational word.

These treasured expressions are given over to the grandchildren and great-grandchildren of W. Myrtle Stewart. Descended through Wilton R. Stewart (spouse Agnes) are Lyle E. Stewart (spouse Lotus) and great-grandchildren Jack and Nina; and Quincy T. Stewart (spouse Angela) and great-grandchildren Annika and Jonah.

Descended through Marquetta R. Stewart (spouse Stephen Matlock) are Jahrod, Jerami (spouse Shaymora) and great-grandchild Cora; and Javier (Spouse Sarah) and great-grandchildren Carter and Emma. Descended through Marquetta R. Stewart (Spouse Michael Brown) is Robin and also, step-daughter Shavonda and great-grandchildren Neveah, Savannah, and Samaya.

Throughout this publication, editing, words of interpretation, and clarifications will be illustrated with the *italicized* term in square brackets (i.e., [ ]).

TABLE OF CONTENTS

THE JOURNEY 7
   BIOGRAPHICAL ACCOUNT 7
      Genesis 7
      Twin Communities 8
      Stage Fright 9
      Oklahoma Journey 10
      Surprise Visit 11
   A GENTLE GIANT 13

1ST MONTH—BEGINNING AND TRANSITIONS .. 15
   PREFACE (MARCH 28, 2010) 16
   NOTING THE AGES (JULY 17, 2014) 17
   GRAND MOTHER'S WRITING (JULY 17, 2014) 18
   PROBLEMS WORKED OUT (JULY, 2014) 20
   TIME BRINGS CHANGE 20
   CHRISTMAS ART 21
   DEEDS FOR THE DAY 22
   NEVER GIVE UP 24
   ON KEEPING BUSY (MARCH 21, 2009) 24
   REPEAT NEAT THREE (JANUARY 21, 2009) 26
   JUST START THINKING 27

Bed Time Stories	27
Everyday Memory Values (2008)	29
Clue (Happy Birthday to Rev. Dr. Art Cribb)	30
End Time Ministries (January 4, 2013)	30
Educational Memory Practice (July 7, 2005)	32
Poem Passion (January 21, 2009)	32
Your Memory (December 12, 2012)	33
Great Number Three (January 1, 2011)	34
Inevitable Number Three! (February 18, 2011)	35
A Three Time Favor (February 18, 2011)	36
4 PM Writing (March 5, 2011)	38
Creativity	38
Just Be Careful (October 31, 2011)	39
Primary Ideas (March 6, 2011)	41
A Willing Partnership (October 28, 2011)	41
November Birthdays (Sister Alice Anna Smith)	42

SHORTEST MONTH ... 43

Great Intentions (October 26, 2011)	43
Courage Values (June 7, 2010)	44
Spirit Lifting Words	44
Good Vegetable Gardens (April 26, 2010)	46
Number Three Values (October 9, 2011)	46
Belated Thanks to Rev. Cribbs (October 8, 2011)	47
Always Feel Free (June 30, 2010)	49
Phenomenal Three Proof	50
Stepping Stones for Richer Zones (November 8, 2012)	51
Extend Your Patience (November 18, 2012)	53

  Self-Control Fruits (June 20, 2010) 54
  Our Beautiful World (1989) .54
  Memory Lane (March 28, 2010) 56
  Happy Birthday Trends (May 2nd, 2009) 57
  Keep on Morning (August 12th, 2013) 62

MONTH OF THE SPRING EQUINOX 63

A MONTH TO PLANT AND GROW 73
  April 8 – My Limerick 75
  Other Kid Memories 76
  April 9 – This is a Limerick About You (about 1965) .76
  Oh Well! So Long They Got Away with It! 76
  Time and Value (June 28, 2012) 80
  Earth, Water, and Sky (December 2, 2008) 80
  On Keeping Busy (January 13, 2013) 85
  The Antique Show 86

THE START OF SUMMER 89
  Memory Class Credits 99

MONTH OF MARRIAGE AND WELL-BEING 103

VACATION TIME 115

HARVEST TIME 127
  Do Your Best 134
  Exceedingly Good Effort 135

>   Grandson's Wedding..........................137
>   There is Magic.............................138
>   Be Careful & Cards 140

INDIAN SUMMER............................**141**
>   Lessons From Two Centenarians..............150
>   The Air Flight 150

AUTUMN MONTH **153**
>   The Antique Show (Revisited)...............156

HUNTING SEASON...........................**165**

WINTER – THE CHRISTMAS SEASON...........**177**

EPILOGUE **191**

APPENDICES **195**
>   Appendix A: Inspiration for A Gentle Giant......197
>   Appendix B: Sisters Story (An April Fool's
>   Day Story) 201
>   Appendix C: Liturgical Dance..................203
>   Appendix D: Mother's Prayer...................207
>   Appendix E: Reflections from Myrtle Stewart...209
>   Appendix F: Childhood Memories That Inspire...213
>   Appendix G: Speeches 219
>   *The Art of Success*.......................219
>   *Impromptu Speech – Homeward*..............220

TABLE OF PICTURES AND FIGURES

Myrtle Edwards in 1941.................................65

Myrtle Edwards in 1943.................................67

Myrtle Edwards – 21 years old in 1938 95

Black Leather Roman Sandal 122

Picture of Board Using Only 2 Players 129

Myrtle – 7 years old 144

Willie Myrtle Edwards – Post Graduate – 1936,
    Douglas High School...............................146

"Rose" Costume......................................162

Myrtle – October 1978, Ah! Ah! 178

Drawing of Anglo-Saxon 187

Marriage Photograph – July 1, 1944 197

Richard & Myrtle Stewart 199

As Adults: Myrtle with three of four sisters
    (Irene not in picture) 201

THE JOURNEY
Biographical Account

Genesis

To begin, this is more than a book of poems written by Willie Myrtle Stewart. It is a life history of a journey taken by an African-American woman who spent 99 years on this planet. The lyrics and memoirs are a window of that journey. Although many of the poems were not written until she was well into her 90s, her interpretation of life experiences serves as inspiration for family, friends, and future generations to admire and cherish. The actual date of creation for some of these poems are listed after the poem title.

Interwoven amongst the original poems are Myrtle's memoirs that were notated in a journal, which she had written throughout a single year as illustrated by inclusive dates. However, the actual year the memoirs were written is unknown. Indeed, Myrtle Stewart was very conscious of the legacy she would leave for others to read. Accordingly, the penned words reflect the diligence she exuded as a very active and prolific writer with a clear memory, which is portrayed in a passage from one of her poems entitled Grand Mother's Writing.

> *I need to leave many points behind,*
> *My family suggested; leave them in rhyme.*

At every opportunity in her last nine years of life, she recorded her experiences in poems and memory passages for others to enjoy. Indeed, at convenient times one could also sit and listen as she read a newly created passage or poem to convey wisdom and remembrance for the captured ear. Serving as interpreters and bibliographers, Wilton R. Stewart, PhD, and Marquetta R. Stewart-Brown, JD, interweave memoirs and poems to create this journey perspective of a fabulous woman who was their mother.

The ensuing sections to this biographical account of Myrtle Stewart's life journey will provide a foundational fabric for Myrtle's poetic tapestry that was delicately created and woven throughout her life. A concluding section (Surprise Visit) to this biographical account affords the ingredients for the first poem you will read, A Gentle Giant by W. Myrtle Stewart.

Twin Communities
Willie Myrtle (Edwards) Stewart, was born on February 26, 1917 in Longview, Texas. She was the seventh of eight children born to Robert "Bob" and Mae Lucy (Craig) Edwards. Myrtle's parents resided on a farm in the twin communities of Pleasant Green and

Greenville in Gregg County, Texas. The farm had valuable woodlands and many fig trees, and the Edwards not only sold cords of wood in the near town of Longview, but also made wooden cross ties for the railroad company. During the months of July and August they sold gallons of ripened figs in Longview. Most of the food consumed by the Edwards family was grown on their farm.

One of Myrtle's fondest memories were of her grandparents, Clayborne Edwards and Alice Ella Wade who resided in the same community. Grandpa Edwards had a grocery store next to Pleasant Green Baptist Church in Longview, Texas. In early childhood, Myrtle attended Pleasant Green Baptist Church under the pastorship of the late Reverend R. B. Francis.

Stage Fright

In June of 1926, when Myrtle was 9 years old, she was in a Children's Day program at Pleasant Green Baptist Church of Longview, Texas. She was scared speechless for speaking. When the time came for her to speak, stage fright took over and her feet took flight. She ran home from church and found freedom under her bed, which was a hilly three miles away. Her dad, Bob Edwards, rushed home, yelling *"Myrtle come out from under the bed; you have embarrassed the family."* Myrtle told her papa that she felt sick. Right soon, he gave her Castor oil. Years passed with this Children's Day program haunting Myrtle who spoke to others and wrote about her regret for running home from church. That memory is well documented in these memoirs.

Oklahoma Journey

Myrtle graduated from Ned E. Williams High School in Longview, originally named Greenville High School, but, renamed after her uncle Ned, who was so well thought of in the community. After graduation from Greenville High School in 1934, her widowed father allowed her to move to Oklahoma City to live with her maternal aunt, Sarah (Craig) Bailey, and attend Langston University. However, she was not permitted to initially attend Langston University because she had not taken Oklahoma history in high school.

When Myrtle started attending church services with Aunt Sarah Bailey, she made acquaintance with other young adults who were students of Douglas High school in Oklahoma City. Subsequently, she enrolled in Douglas High school in Oklahoma City as a post graduate of the senior class to study Oklahoma history and her desired subjects; chemistry, public speaking, drama, and home economics.

In 1936, Myrtle graduated from Douglass High School with honors as an award-winning public speaker. Additionally, during the summer of 1935 and 1936, she and her older sister, Irene, lived in Oklahoma City so Myrtle could save money to attend Langston University. After receiving her second high school diploma, with diligent support from her Aunt Sarah and Sister Irene, she enrolled in Langston University, Langston, Oklahoma, where she was a member of Zeta Phi Beta Sorority. She did miss one semester at Langston University to visit her Aunt Ida Dixon in Depew, Oklahoma. Subsequently, she graduated in 1943 from Langston University with a Bachelor of Science degree in home economics with special studies in education.

Myrtle's first job after graduation was at Shoemake High school, Colbert, Oklahoma in the summer of 1943 as a home economy teacher. At the end of summer, when she returned home to Oklahoma City, her Douglas High school speech and dance teacher, Mrs. Constance Tompkins, offered her a job working closer to home at Dunjee High school in Choctaw, Oklahoma, about 16 miles from Oklahoma City. The principal of Dunjee High was Mr. Abram Tompkins, husband of her speech and dance teacher. Mr. and Mrs. Tompkins lived near sister Irene and could give Myrtle a ride to Dunjee High school daily. From 1943 to 1946, she taught fifth grade classes at Dunjee High School as well her extra curricula jobs including senior Girl Scout Leadership and chairmanship of Junior Red Cross in the wake of World War II emergencies.

Surprise Visit

In 1943, during the Christmas holiday period, Myrtle received a surprise visit from a Sargent Richard Stewart, U.S. Army. When he rang the doorbell, she peeped out carefully saying, "Aren't you lost?" He replied, "*Not really, your college boarding house matron, Bessie Arinwine, is my aunt. She gave me your address and said please visit Myrtle Edwards when chauffeuring your soldier friends from Ft. Sill to Oklahoma City. May I come in Myrtle Edwards?*"

This was not the first time Myrtle and Richard had spoken to each other. It all began in 1942. During Myrtle's attendance at Langston University, she resided in a student home where she was first noticed by a gentleman named Sergeant Richard Stewart, stationed at Fort Sill Army Base in Oklahoma. Myrtle's college residence was managed by Mrs. Bessie Arinwine, Sergeant Stewart's maternal aunt. On occasions, Richard Stewart would visit his aunt Bessie at the boarding house. Out of all the young college ladies living at the boarding house, Bessie's nephew found but one that was most intriguing. However, as far as Myrtle was concerned, he was just Mrs. Arinwine's nephew, a mere acquaintance.

The first poem, A Gentle Giant, commemorates the results of that surprise visit. Appendix A offers the love story that inspired this poem.

THE JOURNEY

A Gentle Giant

March 25, 2006 @ 9:45 pm. Dear Sergeant Richard Stewart, why? Your blood pressure just wants to <u>act up today</u>. Somehow you do not seem disturbed! So, I will just write you a poem.

> My gentle giant, my heart, my love
> We will meet you with our God above.
>
> With our belief you span the sky,
> Like many others you did not die.
>
> I think how you had cared for me,
> As dependable branch on 'Family Tree."
>
> Years passed while I showed appreciation,
> I really feel blessed with God's creation.
>
> I'm sitting here writing (Sgt.), all about you,
> Dear Sergeant, this poem is very true.

[Richard Stewart, a 100% disabled veteran of WWII was a gentle giant. He married W. Myrtle Edwards on July 1, 1944. His word was his bond and his bond was his word. December 17, 1917 – August 8, 2011.]

1ST MONTH—BEGINNING AND TRANSITIONS

January 1

During the month of February on the 26th day in 1917 (i.e., leap year with 29 days), W. Myrtle Edwards was born. I do not remember my mother, Lucy Edwards. She went home triumphant when I was 2 years old. I was told that my baby sister Charlie Mae Edwards was a 10 lb. baby and which made difficult birth for those days. Mother Lucy and baby went home triumphant together. Many people have talked to me about mother Lucy, her sewing ability, her skills and home care. Family: Father Robert Edwards, Children: Robbie Irene Edwards, Marie, Rogers, Alice Anna, Lee Anna, Coila Terry, Willie Myrtle, baby Charlie Mae – The Edwards Family.

January 2

I was born in the "Big Lone Star State" of Texas; 8 miles from Longview, Texas, Gregg County. Area known as East Texas, about 130 mi. west of Louisiana.

Our twin communities were Pleasant Green and Greenville. Our one big united church for all was in Pleasant Green. *[Also located in Pleasant Green was]*[1] Pleasant Green Elementary, Pleasant Green Baptist, Greenville High School.

January 3

I grew up in Longview, Tex. To learn about a Dr. Terry, who delivered my sister Coila Terry (Edwards) Hudson. Since I am only 2 years younger than Coila, I imagine he delivered me 2-26-17 also, and maybe other family members. I was told that Dr. Terry named Coila after his wife Coila Terry. Our grandmother Alice (Wade) Edwards called her "Nap" because of a few nap curls – top her head. Later that nick name was changed to "Cootsy" – My name teasingly "Myrtsy." "Myrtsy" was often used!

Preface
(March 28, 2010)

Writing poems is a blessing for me,
While checking ideas for our family tree.

There are many, many cousins,
When we had parties, they came in dozens.

---

1 Throughout this publication all square bracketed words indicate additions made by the editors (i.e., [ ]).

We had bigtime fun in our own way,
In our big house, all wanted to stay.

Fun was abundant, this was fun,
Many times; just guessing who won!

Noting the Ages
(July 17, 2014)

I am very careful; and trying to see,
All fine things; that could happen to me.

I have worked hard as a young lady,
I am always sure of very good pay, not shady.

Many people work hard for financial pay,
They also make sure trouble stays out of the way!

These notes are good for me to find,
Please read; this is for all mankind.

So, I am scribbling these lines for success,
For I know you are smart enough for the rest!

Grand Mother's Writing
(July 17, 2014)

I have full strength for imagination desire,
This is why I'm writing before I expire.

I need to leave many points behind,
My family suggested; leave them in rhyme.

Yes, I know; no need to tell me,
Family says yes; A good family key!

I thank God that I have enjoyed many years
And my family has helped; erasing all fears.

January 4
Very few photos were taken during my childhood.

January 5 – Brothers and Sisters and Years of Birth [and Death]
1. Robbie Irene (Edwards) Walker, October 31, 1904 – May 7, 1991
2. Marie (Edwards) Johnson, June 2, 1906 – July 1997
3. Rogers Edwards, 1908 – 1930 *[correction, March 12, 1907 – July 2, 1928]*
4. Alice Anna (Edwards) Smith, May 1, 1909 – *[December 12, 2013]*

5. Lee Anna Edwards, 1912? – *[died at age 3, possible year of death is 1915]*
6. Coila Terry (Edwards) Hudson, April 26, 1915 – March 7, 2004
7. Willie Myrtle (Edwards) Stewart, February 26, 1917 – *[March 4, 1916]*
8. Charlie Mae Edwards, 1919 *[Died at birth with mother, Mae Lucy Craig-Edwards]*
9. *[Myrtle's father, Robert Edwards, married his second wife, Dora L. Harris Jamison in 1934]*
10. Everett Clayborne Edwards, *[September 1, 1933 – February 27, 1984]*

January 6

My mother's full name? Mae Lucy (Craig) Edwards *[1885 – 1919]*. Daughter of grandfather Willis and grandmother Anna (Richardson) Craig. Our father's mother and father are Clayborne Edwards and Alice (Wade) Edwards.

In our father "Bob" Edwards *[1880 – 1955]* second marriage, after 15 years a widow, he married Dora Jamison, with 3 children – Cal V. Jamison, Elease Jamison, Addie Lou Jamison, and later Brother Everette Clayborne Edwards was born.

Problems Worked Out
(July, 2014)

Many problems can be worked out,
So, please be without a double doubt.

This a truth for every day,
Yet, don't give up and never play.

While working on some daily troubles,
Solutions may be good as blowing bubbles!

I review these points, often times,
Because it is so easy in making rhyme.

So, I look back on all of these points!
Remembering to dump tobacco joints.

Time Brings Change

Time brings great change
While thankfully dealing with power range.

Please manage to roll with every flow,
Into each graceful day that we know.

Everyone meets their challenges in life,
While we work them in struggle and strife.

We need not stop for any little whim,
So please don't reach a broken limb.

These challenges can get really wise,
And we can get answers without disguise.

Problems tackle everyone on earth,
So please keep a key to successful rebirth!

Christmas Art

It is a fine thing from the start,
To get involved in Christmas Art!

A drop of red and green convey,
A lively spirit every day!

But this alone does not make imparts,
The sweetest of expressive hearts.

January 7

My father's full name was Robert Edwards *[born 1880]*. For some reason he made his signature R.E. Edwards when necessary. He was tall, lean built. We called him Papa, with curly almost straight streaked black and gray hair and mustache, reddish light complexion, wore size 8 shoe. He went home triumphant December 17, 1955 at age 75.

January 8

Mother's date and place of birth? Mary or Mae Lucy (Craig) Edwards. Birth place ____ Texas. *[She went home triumphant]* 1919.

Grandmother Anna (Richardson) Craig married 1880 to Willis Craig (Real name: William Merideth Craig) 1857 – 1940. Worked as a sheriff in Oklahoma State.

Mother Mae Lucy (Craig) Edwards *[was]* 17 yrs. old when she met and married Papa Robert Edwards.

January 9

My father was a carpenter by trade and farming was our best mode for making a living. Food was grown in fields, was clean and pure. One of our best gestures was sharing and borrowing. No one ran out of food. Now-a -days food has some additives.

Deeds for the Day

Did you do your deeds today?
While falling on your knees to pray
For those in need?

I thought about this poem and said,
This entire poem is a deed when read,
With deep sincerity!

1ST MONTH—BEGINNING AND TRANSITIONS

For every moment that we live,
We should practice good service and give
With gracious hands.
This is one way to thank our God,
As we ambulate upon this sod
While we have this time.

Time is element in our lives,
So, we should never give it some jives.
With gracious hands.

This one way to thank your God,
As well as ambulate upon this sod,
While we have full time.

Time is an element in our lives,
And we should never give it jives.
With total exaggeration.

Never Give Up
(For Agnes Lewis, April 19, 1984)

Never give up, give over, or give in,
Strengthen your courage and you are sure to win.

You have seen this happen on other days,
We all know giving up never pays.

When these good thoughts came to me,
I felt this joy of climbing a tree.

This feeling in me was something high
And I checked my steps, to gaze the sky.

Never giving up, makes me feel good,
I show these expressions, in neighborhood.

On Keeping Busy
(March 21, 2009)

Just keeping busy,
Satisfies my mind.
The devil is awaiting me,
To act in ways unkind.

Thanks Westminster Church family for the many blessings that I have received, which tops the list. The beautiful birthday cards so special; the get-well cards. . .

Thank you, one and all.

Richard and Myrtle Stewart

January 10 & 12

When I was a teenager and before I left Texas, I was called "Myrt." My sister Coila was called "Cootsy." People enjoyed being lip lazy. My father's nick name *[went]* from Robert, was "Newt" or "Rob" or "Rock" or "Bob." In fact, Bob Edwards was considered his main name by some people.

Other family nicknames: Irene (Edwards) Walker was Hanna, Marie (Edwards) Johnson was Re, Alice Anna (Edwards) Smith was Ms. Sanna or Sanna, Coila T. (Edwards) was Cootsy and Brother Roger Edwards was Roge.

January 11 – How I Got My Name

My mother named me Willie and later added Myrtle to my name after cousin Myrtle O'Neal of Longview, Tex. One of my sisters says, Myrtle was named Willie after an evangelist minister who visited our Pleasant Green Church often, played piano and sang. I remember Rev. Willie Nixon, Evangelist. He was sort of heavy in statue, clear olive in complexion with curly black hair. Everyone loved to hear him sing.

January 13 – Fathers Style of Living (about 1920-1930)

My father worked in Tyler, Tex. As a candy maker in his younger days. Papa made us taffy candy when we were growing up. He also made peanut brittle and chocolate squares. We helped our Papa maintain successful farming after harvest time in Fall of year. He and our brother made cross wooden ties for the railroad company. We had valuable woodlands. During those days people in Longview used fire place wood; so, Papa cut and sold cords of wood to people in Longview, Tex.

Fig trees surrounded our big bungalow house. July and August were fig ripening time. He sold many gallons of expensive figs.

Repeat Neat Three
(January 21, 2009)

Repeat three times,
While I give rhymes,
Each time I write a verse.

Then you thrive,
You don't miss five,
Take heed, avoid reverse.

Work with number three,
And you will see,
How much its values show.

Just Start Thinking

You can just start thinking,
Good word memory could be sinking,
While living on God's great earth,
Fine things may have rebirth.

Every line I have written is true.
I am happy, while telling you,
These are first I've written today,
Yet I am thinking it will still pay.

Bed Time Stories

It takes only 3 words for good advice,
You may never just say it twice.
You can tell your youngsters again,
But do not make all amends.

We know bedtime stories are very good,
This can be told in any neighborhood.
Yet, please write good thoughts,
Please make sure, nothing ends in ought.

January 14 – The Town I Lived in Before I was 20

[I lived just outside Longview, Texas.] I moved to Oklahoma City when I was 17 yrs. Old. Before I was 17, other towns I visited to see relatives were Marshall, Tex.; Kilgore, Tex.; and Dallas, Tex.

January 15

The childhood addresses that I remember.
1. Family of Edwards: Route 3 Box 86, Longview, Tex.
2. Aunt: 613 N. Eastern, Oklahoma City, Ok.
3. Cousin: Route Box 28, Longview, Tex.
4. Friend: Mary Kate Dunn 4236 N.E. 20th, Oklahoma City, Ok.
5. Myrtle Holloway: 1800 N.E. 11th, Oklahoma City, Ok.
6. Post Oak Community – Our sister Church location
7. New Hope Community Church
8. Red Oak Community Church
9. Elderville, our rivaling White School Settlement

January 16 – A Fond Memory of Grand-Pa *[Clayborne Edwards]*

We really enjoyed visiting Pa's little grocery store, about 40 yards from Pleasant Green Baptist Church, our church. He sold eggs, candy, and canned food. He sold a few other items. Pa sold gasoline for 9 cents per gal. Pa would accept eggs as barter for what some people needed. So as children, we kept the hen's nests cleaned of eggs. Pa Edwards was jolly and full of fun. Everyone loved him because he was always pleasant. He was an olive complexion with wide wavy curly black and white hair and his statue was stocky.

January 17

Grand-Ma Alice *[Wade]* Edwards was a size between 16 and 18. Ma had neck length curly white hair. She was very neat, clean, and very sweet to everyone. I can visualize her in memory, just sitting on side of porch near kitchen and churning milk. Our house was on a slight hill about ¼ mile from her house. In her pantry was all kinds of goods, cookies, honey in combs, and all kinds of fruits.

Ma and Pa's steps were my refuge when I was in trouble. I admired all of Ma's pretty white bridle wreath bushes with white flowers. She grew tamed Dog Wood bushes and Oleander bushes. When I was in trouble on our hill she would yell to Papa, "She is working."

Everyday Memory Values
(2008)

Counting memory values everyday
Can keep valued objects on minds display
While you move on time.

You just need to stop and say
Three times lady; put purse away
Within the closet safe.

Three times these words can give me joy,
So, keep your threes in great employ;
To make up valued time.

Clue
(Happy Birthday to Rev. Dr. Art Cribb)

Your clue fits all economics
So, we need to fan out all comics.

We should make this true ourselves,
And chase away the lazy elves.

We are supposed to be smart in this world.
Showing how, with economics we can whirl.

End Time Ministries
(January 4, 2013)

End time ministries; keep in mind,
Everything that is stated, even online.

It helps people to realize relations,
No matter where they are stationed.

Listen to end time ministries every day,
It helps to know how to keep Satan away.

This is a personal feeling, we should know
While we walk to inform others, door to door.

January 18 – My Favorite Aunt
My favorite aunt was Aunt Fannie Mae (Craig) Patton. She could relate to anything that I wanted to talk about. Aunt Fannie Mae was mother Lucy's youngest sister. Ida (Craig) Dixon was mother's oldest sister. Other Craig family Aunts and [U]ncles: Sarah (Craig) Bailey, Louis Craig, Bob Craig, Joseph Craig, and Addie Craig.

January 19 – Talk About a Favorite Uncle
There were no uncles living in Texas in my mother's family. They lived in Oklahoma. My father's brothers were Uncle Thommy or Tommy and Uncle Clayborne, both deceased before we knew them.

Our well living cousins: Cousin Sicily and Cousin David Jones were our cousins and believing good friends. They were jewels to us. Cousin [Sicily] was a relative from the Bryant family tree relatives of my mother. In our hall way was mother's trunk. Cousin often stopped by on her way to church to wear mother's straw hat. Papa says that mother and cousin Sicily were great friends.

January 20 – Relatives Who Lived with Us
There was a distant relative, his name was Sovola Burnett from Henderson, Tex. He was son of mother's cousin Ella Burnett. We always attended cousin Ella Burnett's church revival in Henderson, Tex. Annually. We saw Sovola Burnett no more after he left our home to run away with one of our cousins, Velma Jones. She was glad when her father Rev. George Jones found her picking cotton with Sovola in West Texas. This was about years 1925 – 1930.

Educational Memory Practice
(July 7, 2005)

Yes, memory is a valued tool
We did not realize this in school.

Somehow, we managed to pass our tests,
While smiling and pounding on our chests.

When value of school is realized late
We need to check what is at stake.

We hope all students today can see
How valued memory practice can be.

Poem Passion
(January 21, 2009)

If you read this poem
You may soon prosper.
Are there better things in life
That we are after?

I believe these words speak for many
All people work for more than a penny.

So, get up, step up and set up,
While collecting poems with you cup

Make them rhyme; all the time,
Even if you need to add a chime.

Your Memory
(December 12, 2012)

Take the time for memory rhyme
While you just have plenty of time.

Check them on non-fading slate,
This, I mean before it is late.

You can do this as "good demand!
To keep, teach truth upon our land.

I am very blessed to bare this time,
To quote good words and make them rhyme.

January 21 – Yes, I had an imaginary friend
This imaginary person was one who could always give me an answer to my unspoken thoughts.

I was taught to believe in Jesus as a friend in every phase of my life. I always remember to talk to Him as a friend.

January 22 – My Correction as a Child
My father Bob always corrected ME, us, even with table manners. We had very tough love. Strict Father

Our community could witness these words above.

January 23 – The Type of Punishment Dealt Me or Us
Papa Bob Edwards used switches, razor straps, or belts if he could find them. You can guess just what happened to these objects. My father looked scary to us when he was angry. However, we had a way with getting away with punishment. He would say, I will get you tomorrow. We tipped around on eggs at a distance from Papa sometimes for days. Grandma Edwards' house was Myrts refuge. "Bob, she is helping me today, leave her."

1ST MONTH—BEGINNING AND TRANSITIONS

Great Number Three
(January 1, 2011)

We have checked; unrealized power of three
The world should listen, as truth to be.

The truth of "Great Earth" should always be credited
So, people can see everything that is still edited.

It is time to place credit where it is due
This powerful, three on earth is noted by a few!

Inevitable Number Three!
(February 18, 2011)

I listen to many speeches almost everyday
While number three is mentioned in an all-inevitable way.

For number three is important, and very hard to miss
I like to listen to speeches in all accomplished bliss.

While making important points to sisters and brothers
We find our talk pointed with three and no other!

__ (This was also penned on February 18, but no title was given for this incomplete poem)

Primary thoughts are my aim
To set up professional game.
Please show that all can describe
While showing additional "chide."

A Three Time Favor
(February 18, 2011)

I asked you three times to drive to the store.
I know you understand; I will not number more.

Three is a striking number, and you must confess,
I have listened to many favors using three and nothing less.

Beautiful number three seams to carry a "special power"
That is why people world over use it every hour.
I am placing double stress on number three, world over,
Number three has more power than lucky four-leaf clover.

January 24

The naughtiest thing I ever did. I tried to work up the soil in father Bob Edwards' cousin Ella Wade's tub of Zina flowers. The seed had already sprouted. I guess I thought I was digging up weeds. I was about 7 years. As a little down the road neighbor trying to help. Cousin Ella (Hollings) Wade was papa's first cousin Walter Wade's wife.

Cousin Ella Wade years later taught me how to make egg custard pie.

January 25 – My Naughtiness Consequences

If I got caught doing wrong of course I would get a good switching. We always managed to stay out of his (Papa's) way long enough and hoping that he would forget. My Papa's biggest punishment was fussing -- and he really could do that. Our forest was full of switches. However, my (or our) Papa liked fussing or talking to us. We dreaded this also.

January 26 – Experience and Memory of a Favorite Cousin

Our Papa's cousin Malinda was one who was also like a mother to us. She was always very sweet. We had to pass her and cousin grant Harper's house to arrive at Pleasant Green Church. She was Malinda (Wade) Harper.

Papa had me celebrating January 26 as my birthday until I was 15 years old. Cousin Malinda says, "Bob. You know that my Daisy Mae is one month older than Myrtle, her birthday is February 26. I know because Lucy and I were expecting at the same time. Remember this was February 26, 3 days before leap year."

4 PM Writing
(March 5, 2011)

In simple life terms you can see,
Just how daily actions affects even me.

If I change simple ideas around,
My office critics would stamp me a clown.
Words inviolable, incredible, renown and unbound,
Are beautiful to hear for particulars in town.

Back to simplify in words I have found best,
I learned this immediately in my intelligence test.

If you can show appeal in your simple writing,
You may brand victorious in your daily sighting.

Creativity

Dignity is noted in columns that bind
With clever anticipation not far behind

Care in using fine words; always good
We experience this often in our neighborhood.

We read, write and be careful of what we say,
Using pen or pencil with other actions display.

Just Be Careful
(October 31, 2011)

Advice – Just be careful is certainly nothing new,
Duty always use this advice to put things smoothly through.

You may always remember in many times passed by.
That you always had success while giving ideas a try.

You need courage from a good stimulating heart
This is a way for creating a very good start.
While looking back, you can always practice in style
Because your special efforts made you happy for a while.

Again – Never give up, give over, nor give in
Using special efforts with talent, sure to win.

January 27 – (Years of 1917, 1919, 1920 – 1930)

I understand that our mother did not work outside of the home. Mother Lucy was a seamstress. I remember that our step mom Dora Edwards did not work outside of home. I cannot remember any of our community women working outside of home unless they were professional people. Farming family life was really something different and women felt that they had all that was necessary to live.

January 28 – Dumb Stunts (1929 & 1930)
When there was nothing exciting to do.

1. Tease wasp nests and run.
2. Tease our mule named "Mag" through our fence to see her kick the fence. Mag was a bad mule.
3. When we had to tie a rope around the baby calf to pull it down the hill to eat grass, it was down a steep hill. Afterwards, we always made the calf snatch us up the hill by placing the rope around our waist. This poor animal was very anxious to get back to mother cow, so helping us climb back up the hill was easy light skips up the hill. This was fun for us.

January 29 – What Coila and Sister Myrtle Fought About Most
My sister Marie Johnson made very pretty dresses for us sisters. She always made us look like twins. If Coila's dress got soiled or damaged I had to watch her to keep her from switching garments, especially socks or anything that looked a little better. She wanted to take it, even if she had no choice (ages 12 and 14 years were trying at times). Coila seemed to create an unexpected attitude. I hope she changed even since 1991.

1ST MONTH—BEGINNING AND TRANSITIONS

Primary Ideas
(March 6, 2011)

Eradicating primary ideas are fine,
But, be careful, don't lose ideas in line.
Cultivating descriptive words in things we do.
Makes multiple interests as long as it is true.

Thanks for any ideas that you have to offer
I find them exceptional and quite ultra-proper.

A Willing Partnership
(October 28, 2011)

A willing partnership is something to admire.
And all willing workers could join this good desire.

So, when you exchange your ideas to make good sense,
They may excite new members to climb over the fence.

Because everyone likes to see jobs growing good,
This kind of interest can excite any neighborhood.

I will say this once, or even say it thrice,
Everyone likes flourishing ideas without rolling dice.

So, join a growing partnership, and don't look back,
Other people can be excited enough to pick up slack

November Birthdays
(Sister Alice Anna Smith)

November cheers, for your sweet years
While birdies tweet, tweet, tweet.
Because everyone knows; your kindness shows!
Through everyone that you meet.

January 30 – Texas Bad Winters

I can remember very cold weather in Texas. Trees covered with ice so heavy the limbs would break. After a big rain, sometimes tree twigs and limbs would hold water that froze over; and when the snow came in winter we did not travel. We liked to tip outside to eat icicles of the twigs. Papa watched us, then say, "Kids, you will get sore throats." However, Papa would make snow ice cream; milk, sugar, and flavoring.

January 31 – Snowy Days

We only read about sledding. We played in snow by falling off large porch into snow. . . . We had to say this was an accident. These were the days that we stayed indoors roasting peanuts that we had a plenty of from our fields. Also, we made popcorn and taffy candy, read stories, and played tit-tat-too.

SHORTEST MONTH

February 1
I remember only one snow man that was made by my brother Rogers once. Papa always kept us indoors during snowy weather. He tried to keep us in good health.

Great Intentions
(October 26, 2011)

The guide of great intentions
May lead to good inventions

Inventions that attract human eye
Which could inspire their workmanship high.

Great inventions are not new
This belief brought world scientist through

Courage Values
(June 7, 2010)

The devil is a busy creature,
He is effective as a sea side lecher,
And if you blissfully get away,
He will try his pranks another day.
A courageous mind is a value to me,
I developed this point for many to see.

Spirit Lifting Words

Please use spirit lifting words
To help sad voices you have heard.

This action will also help you
Because you helped happiness come through.

Sometimes we meet people every day,
Saying, devil took their blessing away.

We could wonder if they are sure,
Or maybe, only, just time demure.

February 2 – Someone I Envied, why?
I envied the girls at Langston University because they always had their mother's photo on their tables in dormitory. These moments needed prayer for lasting recovery.

We envied white children who passed us, making dust in big yellow Elderville High School bus. We were walking three miles to our Greenville High *[School]*.

February 3 (about 1920 – 1930)
Yes, still and all black and white movies were once played at our school. I do not remember who starred in these movies. Mother's first cousin ran these movies.

February 4 – My Favorite Meal as a Child
Chicken, corn bread and greens, just to name a few. We had a wide variety of vegetables in our garden and large fields. My father loved growing eggplant. We raised healthy animals. Also, earth was not polluted as in now. No smog, etc. We had cows, many chickens on our farm. Grandma Alice Edwards had a few turkeys that roamed the nearby woodsy areas coming to coop for evening meals. She raised geese and guinea also.

We had very good food. Guinea was a little grey fowl with tiny white dots. Their meat was dark, unlike hen or rooster.

Good Vegetable Gardens
(April 26, 2010)

Our vegetable garden is very good,
We grow good crops for the neighborhood.

Everyone thinks; this is fine,
Okra, tomatoes, and cabbage – show one of a kind.

We know that veggies are good for our health,
And we should always believe this is a wealth.

Our good neighbors know that this is true,
Because there is no better job on earth to do.

The children of our neighborhood find this fun,
They get more energy to dance and run.

They can buy burger buns; dance and run all day,
But nothing takes good vegetables away.

Number Three Values
(October 9, 2011)

Three is monumental in every place it's shown,
No other number in numerals has passed it in its zone.

With earth, sky, and water around the world we have lived,

Blessings of giving, with a constant giving give.

Be conscious of this blessing, that we enjoy every day,
Everyone is blessed; we dare not fray,
enjoy each day

Belated Thanks to Rev. Art Cribbs
(October 8, 2011)
[This poem was written to thank Rev. Cribbs for his
Eulogy at Richard Stewart's Homegoing Celebration]

I must take time and thank a talented one,
With outstanding talent, under star and sun.

We have held your touching message in our minds,
About a Father and husband joining heaven divines.

We are blessed that our recorded words stated,
So, again, thank you for outstanding honorable words related.

February 5 – My First Finger Smash While Trying to Crack Black Walnuts

Black walnut trees grew wild in our forests, and this kind of tree was always a treasure. Our community knew this walnut was a delicacy. So, everyone had to rush to keep up with the location of trees, the time of their ripening, and when the ripe ones started to fall.

I tried to keep a pile of walnuts outside our house. Sometimes I lightly struck my finger while nut cracking.

February 6 – Famous Person
Reverend Willie Nixon, an evangelist, was a person of whom we said to be famous. I was 6 or 7 years old when he always found lodging at grandma and grandpa Edwards's house. He always performed and ministered rather at our home church, Pleasant Green Baptist, for Longview Tex. Community.

February 7 – One Day Told Papa "Big Fib"
Old Mag, our mule was bad. She kicked me in my forehead. If I had been any closer while teasing Mag the mule, she could have killed me. Of course, I told Papa that I had fallen by our big gate. My older sisters were at school. I was about 6 ½ years old. School age was 7 years. However, I learned to read at a very early age. Papa taught me alphabets and reading before I went to school.

February 8
I did not try to hop a freight train, but I always liked to hear the trains whistle. We always mocked and tried to make a sound like them. I was always thinking that one day I would be able to ride one. Through the still cool country air we could hear that cho! cho! Train.

Always Feel Free
(June 30, 2010)

When you have done your very best,
To prove that you can pass unknown test,
Always feel free.

So, when our lives are filled with tangles,
It is up to us to choose good angles,
And feel free.

Your daily efforts are all about you,
Do not waste time thinking this is not true,
You are free.

Life is beautiful, so take full time,
To thank God for blessings with each clock chime,
You are free.

Stamp out worries; happiness will begin,
There are resourceful challenges awaiting around the bend,
Begin to be free.

So, while blaming yourself, listen to me.
With these lines that you've read, feel free.

Phenomenal Three Proof

Phenomenal three continues to excite me,
But full truth should soon be set free.

If you try very hard in your daily thoughts,
The favorable number three shows without oughts.

So, every day that you watch television,
Number three shows in some speech decision.

Three has a phenomenal practice in daily speeches,
Whether speaking for Godly faith on seaside Beaches.

This worldly number is automatically in front,
Never changes while talking about any stunt.

We need to credit this standard truth anyway,
Because our majestic world is changing every day.

Phenomenal three world may not agree with many,
But we can prove this doubt, without a penny.

Because when many people prepare a special talk,
Memory throws in phenomenal three without a balk.

SHORTEST MONTH

Stepping Stones for Richer Zones
(November 8, 2012)

Stepping stones are always there,
So, take your time; find a stair.

To earn credited daily heights
While flying your colorful daily kites.

These kites show encouraging notes,
While topping districts, wild birds float.

We have a few words only to explain,
How riches are discovered without refrain.

February 9 – Nicknames

I have been called Myrtis, Mary, Mildred, Myrt and anything beginning with M; Myrtle Turdle, Doodle Durdle.

When I was teaching elementary grades (5th) at Dunjee High School in the early 40's, my classrooms back seat row of students would catch me looking aside from them and say very "silly," Mrs. Stew-pot" (for Mrs. Stewart).

February 10 – Nicknames (Cont.)

Some people acclaim poor memory. When I was younger, most times I did not answer.

Some people were also lip lazy.

When I was young, I did not mind.

Some people would say, here comes "Myrtsy and Cootsy."

February 11 – First Boy Friend

Leslie James Coleman. . . We were students at Greenville High School. All we did was look at each other and smile. His cousin, baby girl Coleman was said to be in the Jim Jones Massacre in South America.

February 12 – Valentine's Day

Well, all we did was draw Cupid, darts, hearts, and wish for a program of sorts. All drawings were mounted on class room wall. This alone kept us contesting with each other.

Extend Your Patience
(November 18, 2012)

Extend your patience for any need,
Accept this often, as a fine value creed.

You are helping yours, if by helping others,
This speaks for everyone, yes -- sisters and brothers.

Patience is an excellent word of fine class,
Please review this friend, and make it vast.

Sometimes we don't say this enough,
So just keep it up; wear it on your cuff.
When our minds have meaning demure,
Then, we can watch double action for sure!

Self-Control Fruits
(June 20, 2010)

There are fruits in self-control,
To value happiness untold.

You can miss a slap in your face,
Which could make you a hospital case.

This is making a frightening verse
Which is looking like a devil's curse.

But if we watch our steps each day,
The fruits of wise thoughts can pay.

Our Beautiful World
(1989)

Our huge world is a beautiful place,
It's magical beauty shows saving grace.

I walk down paths of pebbles and thrills,
To photo rocks upon the hills.

I take them home and wash them clean,
To record them with my nightly dreams.

I chose these words, crafted at the best,
To puzzle my readers to guess the rest.

> I collected pebbles, sticks, and large rocks,
> Placed fall time red leaves in my socks.
>
> I like walking near our large meadows,
> To gaze at side trees with long shadows.

February 13 – A Special Valentine

We always drew ♥'s *[hearts]* for our favorite teacher. Our young lives were very simple to the point that we were not excited enough to do anything like children and grown-ups of today. No television. No news reports. All communications came from school and church. We can look back and say how we were hampered. We knew no different, like many more.

February 14 – Special Valentine (Cont.)

I did not remember receiving special valentines when I was a child or even after *[I]* was older; maybe after I enrolled at Douglas High in Oklahoma City, after meeting classmate Alvin Faine. I learned *[in]* later years that he became a minister. He was a football player for Douglas High in the 30's.

February 15 & 16 – My First Kiss?

I do not remember a kiss from my new friend Alvin Faine, just maybe however. He was a quiet one also. I was a post graduate at age 17. I wanted to or needed to take more science. I enjoyed Douglas High drama classes which proved to be fruitful for me. I can say that I was slightly afraid of boys. First dates were like a dream. In Texas everyone we met were cousins. So, a high school mate, Curtee Roberts, wanted to take me to a school dance (our senior year). We had too many distant relatives. Sure enough – Curtee Roberts (who had a twin brother Curtis) with an acclaimed distant father, was our relative. So, this date changed tunes.

Memory Lane
(March 28, 2010)

While walking down memory lane,
I needed a good walking cane.

I did not need to chance myself a fall,
Memory needs attention, even when walking tall.

Walking gives us a precious time to think,
Valuable thoughts have time to sink.

I choose a special valley in which I like to prance,
This gives my body exercise with memory advance.

SHORTEST MONTH

Happy Birthday Trends
(May 2nd, 2009)

[This poem was written on the occasion of the 100th birthday of Myrtle's sister, Alice Anna.]

Hello to all relatives, members, and friends,
We know you are here for birthday trends.

My speech may seem sorts funny---
But I really hope it is on the money.

We are celebrating a birthday 100,
Relatives and friends may be in a wonder.

And sister Alice you were always great,
I always read this on my slate...

Just how you taught me beautiful craft,
Demanding my attention like an army draft.

In my family, I am member number seven,
Our parents, with other members, are in heaven.
(Father Robert Edwards and Mother Lucy Craig Edwards)

I don't know why I tell you this. . ..
But our grandniece Jennifer Williams is a special bliss...

She emailed all the ideas that she could,
She is a very smart lady; we know that she would.

Thank you, Marquis, Jennifer Williams, and baby America, too,
Just keep the faith, your reward is coming through.

My sweet daughter Marquetta Brown with granddaughter
Robin and I,
While joyfully smiling, and getting on South West plane to fly.

I wrote this speech in poetry, for writing poetry is my game,
When you are age 92 you may like to do the same.

Again, thank you one and all,
For you have witnessed Sister Alice's 100 birthday call.

February 17 – [Television Shows]
My first TV shows; "Little Rascals", later years "A Men."
Black and white movies were a scattered few in some places in late 30's and 40's and before 1920 – 1930.

February 18 – Family Reunion in My Childhood
First Sunday in August was celebrated annually at our Pleasant Green Baptist Church. With 50 or 60 families meeting with home coming family members from far away towns, etc. This was also Annual Revival Week. Outstanding ministers were invited to speak. All families brought trunks and huge boxes of food. Tables were set up on church grounds and everyone tried to find a shade tree to set up dinner tables. Many people attended and had to taste each cousins' food. Everybody wore new clothes. During this revival and reunion, half of these people never walked inside

the church building nor hear the Christian services. Truthfully, some young and old walked the dusty roads to eating tents, *[talk to]* each other and made photos. The first Sunday in August is still popular.

February 19 – My School Days

I had to be 7 years old before I started Pleasant Green Elementary. This was 8 months after I was to. This was school board idea. That was OK, my papa taught me alphabets and figures. I could read the primer book when I enrolled in school. There was a Blue Book speller at my house, I guess it got burned in the 60s. I remember that Blue Book speller is collector's item with value today. I learned some English corrections, some proverbial *[passages]* and poems when we had this book at home. I enjoyed the inspirational verses in this book.

February 20 – My Least Favorite School Subject

Algebra of course. I think the problem was with the teacher. No one wanted to teach algebra at our school. I really feel cheated because this subject was dumped on our home economy teacher Edna Mae Jacobs and she showed her disinterest by giving her least assistance and attention. I was a pretty good math student, but every civil service exam that I have had introduced algebra problems. Poor teachings set me back in math especially. . . Our chances were not promising in our schools in Texas.

February 21

I had problems with math in 7th grade. I felt proud of myself. However, when I worked a math problem which had eight angles and eight sides, my teacher cousin Ambrose Taylor did not believe that I worked the problem. (I stayed up most on one night). I was the only one in class that work*[ed]* the octagon figure problem. Cousin Ambrose Taylor was a very good teacher.

February 22 – Jr. High School Problem

Yes, I had problems again *[in]* junior high. I had a poor teacher; Edna Jacobs. This is one subject that I really needed to know – a big career setback for me. I also needed to be more aggressive.

February 23 – Senior High School Problems

My biggest problem was walking to school. While Elderville High School students bus passed us whenever we were walking three miles to Greenville High in the rain, near Longview, Texas.

February 24 – 1920 & 30s Hopes and Dreams, Longview, Texas

I enjoyed going to Ma Edwards home when I was a child at home in Texas. I liked sitting by the creek fishing while I thought of my hopes and dreams and meditate*[d]*. Our big bungalow house in woodsy acre; sitting on long L [shaped] porch in moon light watching shooting stars and making a wish. I liked going in our forest to pick wild violets – many wishes were made.

February 25 – The 1930s, Secret Creek Leaping Game

Secret Creek Leapers: Rosie Britton, Lorena Wright, Elizabeth Borders, Coila T. Edwards, Myrtle Edwards, Geneva Borders, and others as score keepers. Yes, there was a clear creek branch of water running backside of Greenville High campus. At long lunch hour instead of playing softball, we found time to tip downhill and have a clear creek jumping contest. (Girls only). No pants worn these days. This creek – 4 or 5 feet wide, but it was fun to wear the full flair skirt dress just to see it flair when in jumping contest. Yes, tail got wet sometimes. Girls would twig beat dress tail dry before bell rang for back to class room work. Teacher Edna Mae Jacobs finally caught up with our recess game. Yes, she punish*[ed]* us.

February 26 – Early 1930s, A Good Hangout Place?

Hangout were not a good thing for us. When at church there was a long trail to a spring beside of a hill, and young people stayed thirsty enough to find a way to chat and walk just for social times together. Shade tree or benches were at our convenience.

Keep on Morning
(August 12th, 2013)

Prayerfully keep morning known
You may find yourself in blessed zone

This is not just printing nice word
But, taking advantage of speeches heard.

When you listen to good word talk
It may make old Satan change his walk.

To write these good words every day,
Surely keeps a good spirit on your way.

February 27 – The Best Pet I Ever Had

Our family pet was slick red hair Mary, our pretty general horse. Coila and Myrtle could ride to the branch of water barebacked to watch her drink. We would hold to her long mange to keep from falling off. Ma and Pa Edwards had two pretty dogs – "Shep and Prince." We caught and played with wild birds sometimes also. Caught butterflies for their pretty wings also.

February 28 – 1920 – 1930 – Other Pets We Had

Between 1925 and 1930 we always claimed the prettiest chickens in one yard. The little baby chicks would peck crumbs from our hands before the[y] knew that they were grown to be eaten. Grand parents' dogs; we loved them too. Prince was a small smooth white dog with brown spots. Shep was a big shaggy white dog with large black spots.

MONTH OF THE SPRING EQUINOX

March 1 – School Programs
The programs and plays that we were in mostly, school closing and special occasions, and of course holidays. Our sister Marie always made pretty white dresses *[for]* school closing. New clothes for all special occasions. Papa always bought very good shoes. Our main programs included singing and memorizing poems.

March 2 – School Principal
Uncle Ned *[E.]* Williams, Principal of Greenville High later named Gregg County Teaching school. In recent years the new name of N. E. Williams High School. This change was in uncle Ned's honor. N. E. Williams was considered one of East Texas' famous educators. He was our uncle by marriage to our mother's aunt Ada (Richardson) Williams.

March 3
I like*[d]* school so much more than one could think. Of course, I found a good way to stay out of fall field harvests, appealing that

some school days were special days for me. I had inspiration but with no tools or special help. Our teaching system was held back by segregation.

March 4 – About Cussing?

Yes, I made the mistake of calling my papa a fool. I did not know that he heard me. You can imagine the consequence. He asked stepmom Dora if she heard me just to verify what he heard. She said yes. Our father was a good person; yet, at times he was too fussy.

March 5 – Spending Saturday Time

I spent my Saturdays studying school assignments, cleaning clothes, and preparing for church attendance. We, Coila and I, always *[studied for]* school and church at the edge of our shady forest, made mud pies in fruit jar tops and served these pies to our rag dolls. *[We also performed]* speech making while stand*[ing]* on tree stumps.

March 6 – Spending Sunday Time

My church going was spent like most youngsters; we had new clothes for all occasions. Sometimes we visited cousin Ella Burnett in Houston, Texas about 25 miles away. Their revival was a later date in August at Antioch Baptist.

March 7 – Meanest Thing I Did

One evening after school one "meanie" girl student *[meant]* to get a bad bluff on sister Coila T. When she (Lorena Wright) thought that she had made her bad bluff on Coila T., she turned around to get slow moving Myrtle. Lorena met my heavy rimmed lunch pail in her face. This was a surprise that I hope she never forgot.

March 8 – The Consequences from March 7 Story (about 1925 – 1934)

I do not remember what happened after this incident. I hope she realized that the slow quiet people are also not to be taken lightly or for granted. . . Tip around them lightly is better. I called myself the "Slow Unassuming Winner."

March 9 – Radio Programs

My style or type; symphony or opera type music on radio. I listened to Amos and Andy and Kingfish. Opera music gave me a certain kind of high. As a child, like others, this type of music helped me with my dreams. There was little else to do except dream and wish!

March 10 – My Favorite Movie? (1920 – 1930)

We saw very few movies while growing up. A few black and white silent movies were played at our school. There were theatres with balcony seating for Blacks in Longview, Texas. I am sure that the entire south was the same.

Myrtle Edwards in 1941

March 11 – Did Kids Ever Tease Me? (1925 – 1930)

Yes, Sisters and friends had to have someone to tease. I was called "Myrtle, Turtle, Doodle Durdle." *[They would be]* clowning around and lick-out their tongues. I say only to make themselves feel better. Just to make an ugly face at me was sometimes demeaning to me as a child until I was taught what to do.

March 12 – School Essays: Difficult? (Early 1940s)

English teacher, Hobart Jarriet, from New York area taught English at Langston. He was very strict and hard to please. Tall, neatly dressed, nice suits *[with]* stiff collared shirts and bow tie. Hobart walked and talked like he thought someone was constantly taking a photo of him. Very few as in his class, if any. We had much respect for Jarriet. We felt that we had a teacher who cared for our future.

March 13 – First Smoke

Some moments at work were dull and tiresome. (Terminal Annex Post Office). I tried to smoke since smoking was not illegal at that time on the job. Ashtrays were even given to anyone who desired to smoke. I *[soon]* found very little interest in smoking. Chewing gum became *[my]* new habit. Poem writing during coffee break besides gossiping *[also became a habit]*.

March 14 – My First Pizza

Yes, thought that my first pizza was too doughy. So, I started making my own pizza. I made pizza often for Westminster

Presbyterian *[church]* for fellowship hour. Everyone thinks I am a good pizza cook. My brother Everett started to making pizza. Everette C. Edwards was *[a]* short order cook at Harrah's Restaurant *[in]* Reno, Nevada.

March 15 – College Choice

Myrtle Edwards in 1943

I chose Langston University *[located]* 40 miles from Oklahoma City. It was convenient for me to travel home to sister Irene E. Walker's *[home]*. My sister Irene meant everything to me and totally responsible for my chance to go to school in Oklahoma. Irene's neighbors were Mr. and Mrs. Abram Tompkins. Mrs. Tompkins was my speech teacher. When I finished at Langston, she helped me get a teaching job at her husband's school.

March 16 – My college Major

My mother Lucy was a seamstress. She made clothes for people. I grew up with a creative mind to sew and do crafts. When I majored in home economy at Langston University, my home economics teacher, Edith Tate from Atlanta, Georgia, gave me credit for explaining what home economics meant *[to me]*. My answer was "take what you have and make what you want." Mrs. Tate liked this answer. This inspiration heightened my spirit.

March 17 – St Patrick's Day
We were green on St Patrick's Day and drawing shamrocks was fun. We always tried to find a four-leaf clover in *[the]* adjoining meadows, thinking of good luck with odd leafed clovers.

March 18 – St Patrick's Day (cont.)
This was one day that went unnoticed by many Americans. This was an Irish holiday. During my work at post office, we teased workers who forgot to wear green on March 17.

March 19 – No Hitch-hiking
We were taught that hitch-hiking is dangerous. We rode with no one except relatives. We respected this demand from papa.

March 20 – My Favorite Time of Year
I was very sad when I learned the truth about Santa Claus, Easter, and Christmas. Santa Claus is you mom and dad, and Easter bunnies do not lay eggs. This was a truth that I did not want to accept.

Christmas was my favorite time of year. We always found and kept our boxes ready for months. Mostly shoe boxes. We received mostly the goodies and confections not seen before December.

Dried raisins on long stems, apples and oranges, and nuts of all kinds. . .. Dolls also. Once we found hidden candy in our garage before Christmas. I don't know how long Coila had been eating candy before Christmas.

Our big sisters always made Easter eggs and hid them in our big vegetable garden.

March 21 – Household Chores
Dish washing was done with sister Coila soaking all of her pots and pans for next-time dishwasher, whose name was "Myrt." We had wood burning heaters so we had to go to wood stack and pack wood in for the winter evenings. We packed water from springs that was located down-hill about ½ block. The forests had no pollution.

March 22 – Outside Chores
Picking fruits like figs, peaches, and plums. Working in cotton fields *[was also an outside chore]*. However, *[before picking cotton,]* earlier we had to trim the cotton rows of grass and weeds, while thinning the cotton plants. Sweeping our yard with handmade dog wood brooms. We sometimes helped our grandma call the cows from pasturing; *[singing]* "soo cow ♪, soo cow ♪."

March 23 – My Disliked Chores
It seems that our so-called chores were too drastic to be anything except hard work or hard jobs. We disliked field work. Dish washing was hard because we had to pack water. Our well always ran dry.

March 24 – Broken Bones (year about 1925)

I have never had broken bones. However, I received a forehead cut above my eyes while running from ma's mean cow; named Meaner. I was about 7 or 8 years old and I tried to duck under a low barbed wire fence. The barbed wire cut me on my forehead. We were not teasing Meaner. She just expected us to tease her. Ma Edwards treated my bleeding head.

March 25 – I did not need stiches.

When I fell on a nail head half hammered into a very thick step board, the nail cut my lip on lower right corner of my mouth. A small scar is still slightly seen. I also cut my foot with a hoe accidentally. Grand-ma Alice (Wade) Edwards treated us from her box type table medicine cabinet.

March 26 – Injury Stories

We had 4 or 5 fig trees in our back yard that stayed full of this delicacy. I fell out of a fig tree, knocking breath out of myself. Sister Alice came running, Myrt, Myrt! All at once hearing her, I hopped up and ran into our house. I did not stop climbing that tree, but I did learn to hold to limbs. Papa sold figs. They were expensive.

March 27 – Child hood Illness

As a child I had roseola, measles, and terrible colds in cold Longview, Texas until I was 17 years old. Papa would give us Castor oil or Black-Draught for colds. That stuff was very hard to swallow. When we got a wee chance, we would slyly pour it out. Black-Draught looked like dried ground oak leaves. Castor oil was a clear sticky substance that had to be heated and taken by table spoon. These medications would take you to the bathroom quickly.

March 28 – Experience at the Doctor's (about 1922)

I had to visit our Dr Terry for some reason; illness? Near the month of December Doctor Terry wanted to know what I wanted for Christmas. I named so many toys (I am told) until Dr. Terry became deaf to my wishes. Dr. Terry named sister Coila Terry after his wife. I understand he liked being our family doctor.

March 29 – My Best School Charm

Rebecca Sanders, Verdee Garret, Georgia Mae Borders, Naomi Harper, Ola Mae Fowler, and Ollie Taylor. Most of these girls were our relatives. March 30 – Crazy Nicknames

Naomi Harper was Noma, Daisy M. Harper was Boo, Coila Terry Edwards was Cootsie, Myrtle Edwards was Myrt, Valarie Portley was Pugga, Esterlena Wade was Shang, Alice A. Edwards was Sona, and Irene Edwards was Hanna. The Edwards' girls were Edards girls and Dr. Robert L. Harper was called Woody.

March 31

We once took two hairpins with a rubber band attached between the pins, twisted the rubber fully, carefully placed in in a single folded paper. Placed it in a small envelope, sealed it and wrote a family members name on it and tell them to open it. . . A big flutter is experienced before it can be thrown down. We played this joke on Papa once. . . he was a good sport.

A MONTH TO PLANT AND GROW

April 1 – April Fools' Day[2]

About 1931 or 32 Papa wanted to get even with our step-mom Dora. He placed a large humped stick across the road in front of our house. . . threw his black over coat over the humped wooden stick. Then he loaded his gun, hid, and told us to shoot the gun. After Mrs. Dora sees the black coat, she screamed, "Oh! We done shot Mr. Bob. We were scared and we shot Mr. Bob, Oh!" (See Appendix B.)

April 2 – Jokes and Pranks

My sister Coila use*[d]* to hide in our large hall way at home. She knew that I would make a quiet nights' visit to the food pantry, and she scared the day-lights out of me. Yes, believe it or not, I was really plump for *[my]* figure. Coila was devilish and skinny and mischievous.

---

2 Myrtle Edwards recorded a second April Fool's Day Story entitle "Sisters" that was discovered in her written documents. See Appendix B for the "Sister" story.

April 3 – What I wanted to be When I Grew Up

I wanted to be a musician at first. I thought strongly about nursing profession from Papa's encouragement. But home economy studies were more interesting in the 1940 years when I went to Langston University. I did very well with oratory. As an elective I won $100 in a speaking contest at Douglas High School, Oklahoma City. I also won a trip to Prairie *[View]* University in a speech contest in 1933.

April 4 – Kite Making?

We made paper sails that did not sail very high. We just folded large papers and threw them in the air. This was not much fun for girls. Our cousin Eldrige Price would visit Ma Edwards from Dallas, Texas and bring his kites and toys. We helped him enjoy them.

We had fun telling Eldrige that Ma was closer in relation to us than to him; she was Grand Ma. He would run to her crying. She would tell him, "You, Eldrige are great and grand."

April 5 – Experience with Kites

We had the kind of paper sales [sic] that we did not mind losing in the trees. We always felt very sorry when cousin Eldrige's kites got hung on telephone lines and hung in trees. Eldrige was 2 years younger than Myrtle.

April 6 – Wild Animals

We tried to trap wood or tree squirrel. We trapped black birds in our barn. The seeding barn attracted black birds after harvest. Black bird breast was our delicacy. We tried to catch little rabbits also. Wild animals are hard to keep alive in captivity. . . They do not live long.

April 7 – Yes, We Tried to Adopt a Wild Animal

Coila and I were always catching red birds and blue birds. Sometimes little wren birds. These birds would not eat because of fear; we were sorry to see them die. We kept some small rabbits a while. It was always fun to find a bird nest of pretty little eggs. We tried not to touch them.

April 8 – My Limerick[3]

They said, "Myrtle, Turdle, Doodle, Dirdle,
And people seemed out of mind.
Asked my friend to do the hurdle,
This new crap, not in her time.
"Country life dealt big mud-puddles"
Jumping sticks fell out of line.

---

3   A limerick is a humorous nonscience verse of five anapestic lines.

Other Kid Memories

What we going to do for bacon now?
Sambo shot the "Sandy Sow."
She jumped the fence and broke a rail,
Sambo shot her through the tail.

April 9 –
This is a Limerick About You
(about 1965)

Willow did better,
When chance to show his pride.
So, friends and foe let hiss
Then dropped their heads and cried
Far wanted even ties.

Oh Well! So Long
They Got Away with It!

Marquetta and Wilton liked playing piano,
They practiced daily for winning banner.
At dishwashing time piano was fun,
This was no way to get jobs done.

April 10 – A Favorite Spring Memory
We enjoyed picking pretty wild flowers notable for East Texas. Easter time with all the flowers that we had to decorate our church; especially Lilly plants. We always had new clothes and plenty of pretty Easter eggs that we thought rabbits laid in Papa's big garden.

We learned Easter speeches, sang Easter songs, and always did a lot of marching.

April 11 – Mom nor Dad Found Nothing that We had Hidden
Sister Coila always found my movie magazines to tell Papa about them; why, I do not know. Coila was a busy body for aggravating me. I think she didn't like to see me so contented at times. Age difference (that is 2 years) I guess which did not make a big difference with me. So "sham battles grew!"

April 12 – Some Church Memories
I once was scared speechless for speaking on Children's' Day program. I ran home from church on Children's' Day in June about 1926. I told Papa that I felt sick. Right soon, he gave me Castor oil. I regretted my running home from church. I must have been about 9 years old.

April 13 – Memory About a Church Social Activity
This was not said to be so social; however, people made it so. Our church officers worked hard to find the best Christmas speaker for saving souls. I remember how my sister Marie and cousin

Jerusha Jones made beautiful clothes for everyone on Home Coming Sunday. Some of these people did not enter the crowded church. The dusty road was like a fashion parade as people strutted from one eat stand to the other. The Robert "Bob" Edwards was no different. The Pleasant Green Baptist Church Revival dinner was served from [a] truck or big box under [a] shade tree and under tent.

April 14

Our sister Alice and Marie Edwards were older than Coila and Myrtle. (There was a deceased sister next to Alice in age that we were too young to know. Her name was Leeanna). We had older sisters that were nice and sweet enough to decorate eggs and place them in our Papa's Garden among the Sweet pea vines. I was very unhappy when sisters got tired of surprising us. . . They said, "Rabbits did not lay the eggs, we placed them in Papa's Garden."

April 15 – Easter Sunrise Service, No

There was no Sunrise Services for Easter. There was a regular 9:00 AM Sunday School with Children's program for Easter, while other Easter services followed during the day. Papa always bought us new clothes. Marie made new dresses. I remember a very pretty pink crepe-de-chine dress made for me. Coila's dress was deep American beauty Rose in color.

April 16

Other Easter traditions included song practicing and speech memorizing for Easter Sunday. We knew that this was all necessary to help us show off our new clothes.

April 17 – When We Played Make Believe and Pretended (1924 – 1926)

Coila and I played housekeeping outside under the big shade trees around our house. Dirt mud pies, a specialty, we pretended eating this junk. Sometimes our cousins Sophia and Jennie Wade played mud cook-out in play house with us. We also had preaching service while standing on three stumps in front of our house; singing and moaning was in order.

April 18 – If I Could Return to My Childhood

The first thing I would do is practice memory comprehensively. I would know how to remember valuable information by practicing and by associating valuable and interesting information with things and names (i.e., already familiar). I would begin with math and history. I would put more time in English.

I would also ask my father to buy corrective shoes for me. My shoes were always too short.

Time and Value
(June 28, 2012)

You must keep this in mind,
Practice progress while you're speaking,
While thankfully earning a time.

Use time as your stepping stone,
With monuments every day,
This can show you're good value prone.

We need to create good works in rhyme,
To prove a certain point,
Good works are models in time.

Earth, Water, and Sky
(December 2, 2008)

We have earth, water, and sky,
A threesome group man can't deny.
It is a huge blessing of God's creations,
Encouraging repentance with saving relations.

April 19 – I would Try to Do Differently as a Teenager

Yes, I would be careful how I wear my shoes. Read more good books for vocabulary development. Do more poem writing for inspiration; although I tried, with opportunities exposed to me. I cannot complain. . ... Somethings [sic] in life can be changed to our liking, others cannot. There is an art of living. . ... Adjustment and readjustment, and it is accomplished by self.[4]

April 20 – I Wrote Poems When I Was a Teenager

Yes, I wrote poems of fields and streams when I was a teenager. There was always something about babbling brooks and running streams of water that fascinated me. In fall of year tree leaves of gold, yellow and red gave me a feeling to make rhymes. I am sorry that I did not keep them. In 1994 this write up was enjoyed. Our church Westminster Presbyterian witnessed an outstanding writing about liturgical dance. First Chronicles, Chapter 13, 15, and 16 it seems that David danced before the Lord with enthusiasm. Article about churches liturgical dances by Myrtle Stewart was written. Our praise dancer is Leuer Aasen, my friend. (See Appendix C).

April 21 – Books Read as a Child

I was attached to my 1st grade primer. The children's pictures are still in my mind. I could not go to school until my 7th birthday. My 1st birthday was February 26. So, I always felt that I was

---

[4] The name Leroy Brownlow was penned to the end of this sentence. This passage of words may have been something written by another author.

cheated out of one full semester. I loved the primer book and the Blue Back Speller (now collector's items). I believe that teachers got tired of skipping me out of their class. Papa had taught me alphabets and I learned to read all billboards when we were going places. Papa taught alphabets forward and backwards. I can say them backwards correctly to this 84th year.

April 22 – My Biggest Physical Problem

I have had to deal with feet problems. Shoes have been bought too short in the past. I should have had corrective shoe wear or foot wear. I believe my mother would have cared for my shoe fitting problem.

April 23

Father Bob Edwards taught us against superstitions. He told us about one can clicking against other cans that were tied together when the door to grand-father Clayborne Edwards' cannery house door was opened. Some people would say, "There is a ghost in the cannery. Sometimes glowing phosphorus in fresh plowed soil could be seen at night. . . We were taught that this was only a chemical *[reaction]* and not some ghost action.

April 24 – Our Best Hide and Seek Places (1920s)

Our best hiding hide-and-seek places were behind large trees, behind pap's chicken house, and behind our horse's stable and barn. This time in my life was enjoyable as a child and in some ways fruitful. . . In that I have learned to be thankful more and more.

April 25 – The First Time I Was Behind Wheel of Car

When I was 13 years old my brother Rogers Edwards left car keys in our 1926 Ford (at that time a popular model). I hopped in the Ford and drove a few yards. When just before I arrived at a big gate my brother hopped in and took over the Ford. I wanted to drive. My older sisters could drive. The only chance for my driving again was in 1945, after my husband Richard Stewart went overseas to war in Europe.

April 26 – Taking Something That Was Not Mine (between ages 13 and 15)

Yes, it was bees' honey. Robbing bee hives in pa Edwards' fruit orchard. I generally tipped out of ma's sight with a hammer and a knife, just to tap on pa's bee hives to make the bees crawl to the bottom of the cage or hive. Good! Then, I could cut a big chunk of honey and eat it while out in pa's fruit orchard. Ma could have been asleep. Also, we liked finding pennies in ma's pantry. . . The most interesting place is ma's house; there were all kinds of goodies. I do not think that ma cared. She wanted me to be happy with adventure.

April 27 – I Did Not Get Caught Robbing for Bees' Honey

I ate honey, fresh honey is very good eaten from the waxed comb. The bees always filled out the fresh trimmed honey in the hive boxes before it is noticed. I always placed top of bee hive back and tapped it back together. I can see the pear and peach orchard across road from ma's house. I just smile because I knew how to settle the bees down for safety.

April 28 – Many Years Later, December 1943

I know a story about a big surprise in Oklahoma City. The biggest surprise that I can witness was made by someone that I met at Langston, Oklahoma about two years earlier, while they were visiting a relative. While I was enjoying holiday break (in 1943) from Dunjee school classroom. (Had flue cold). I was also shut in by sister Irene who had gone to work. (Near Christmas) someone knocked at the door. Who *[was it]*? He says, "Sgt. Richard Stewart." Uncle Rogers and Aunt Bessie had a bet that I was going to marry Minas Campbell. My school matron from Langston *[Bessie]* settled the bet by sending Richard Stewart to my house. Once he saw that I was ailing with a cold, he left quickly and returned with a large bag of fruit. I said, "What does all of this action have to do with me." "Well," he says, "I would like to buy you a house." I of course struck a slow smile. I gave this story some thought. We have been married 57 years. We married July 1, 1944. (Today's date as I write is May 20, 2001).

Christmas Day – December 25, 1943

A beautiful white snow had covered the ground. Myrtle Edwards could not dare go outside as cold as it was *[because of]* a touch of flue. Sister Irene says, "I bought you some snow boots. *[Myrtle says,]* "Thank you, I am expecting Sgt. From Fort Sill, Oklahoma to visit me." Knock, knock. Stewart enters and says, "Hello Myrtle, how are you feeling." His beautiful eyes edging from his barracks cap, smooth and straight khaki uniform. When I was ready to say, "I am feeling just fine," sister Irene says, "She wants to visit our aunt Fannie Mae Patton and family but don't you think it is too cold today?" Sgt. Stewart says, "her feet does [sic] not have to touch the ground." And at that moment he picked me up and put me in his car and drove me 16 miles to Parkers' Heights in Choctaw, Oklahoma to visit Aunt Fannie Mae Patton, Uncle Legus Patton and his beautiful family. The whole family fell in love with Richard. Sister Irene even sent him shirts on my birthday. There is more. And how Sgt. Richard managed to drive to Oklahoma City every weekend I do not know.

On Keeping Busy
(January 13, 2013)

On keeping busy is a great thing
Adjusting to problems is enormous ding.
I set my feet out on the street
Awaiting for new people I'd like to meet.

The Antique Show[5]

The antique show,
Of interest for many to go.
To witness objects old fashion,
By many people with labeled action.
Antiques have shown many years,
For everyone with antiquated peers.
They find antiques in great-grands cabinets,
That will turn heads while recording all on tablets.
Valuable antiques show we do inspire,
We show surprise while we admire.

April 29 – Childhood Fears Remembered

Some sleeping time nightmares. . . Before my father completed the building of our house, the girl's bedroom had no complete ceiling for a while. There seemed to be a goat with horns looking down on me. Sometimes when I was asleep, it seemed that the main hall door was opening when it was supposed to be locked. I remember awakening with a scream.

April 30 – Dunjee High School: A May Day Tradition (1942-1944)

When I was a 5th grade teacher, *[an]* 8th grade history teacher, and

---

5   This is the first of two poems that Myrtle Stewart wrote with the same title. The Antique Show (revisited) appears later in this publication.

[a] home room teacher at Dunjee High in Choctaw, Oklahoma, we had the classes wrap the flag pole with spring-colored ribbons. Each class would have different colors of ribbon to wrap a pole within a time limit while band music was played. This was an afternoon event with parents visiting.

Dunjee High School was named for Roscoe Dunjee, Oklahoma City's Black newspaper reporter. He was recognized as a concerned community care giver in Choctaw, Oklahoma (Parkers' Height addition, [which was located] 16 miles from Oklahoma City, Oklahoma).

THE START OF SUMMER

May 1 – May Baskets, What They Contained
We made baskets from card board as children. However, by the time the basket was filled with wild poses and daises, ferns, etc.; *[the]* basket was falling apart. Our straw sun hats were always floppy and *[contained]* bent wild flowers also. Wild violets were very many in our community. . . Blue Bells, Fox Glove, and Sheep Sorrel Blossoms. Sheep Sour leaves had a tangy sour taste. Wild onions were tasty also, while holding to our over filled baskets. Shang Weeds were pink with fragrant smell – with leaves lacey that would fold up when touched.

May 2 – The Price of Ice Cream Cones (about 1924 – 1925)
I remember paying .10¢ and .15¢ for an ice Cream cone! Our father made ice cream often. We had a plenty of milk. Many ready prepped foods that we buy today – We prepared ourselves from our <u>organic fields</u> home dairies. These foods were pure. Every neighbor had their own "smoke house" for curing and storing meats of all kinds. People bought only what they could not produce.

May 3 – Tree Houses

We did not have a tree house. We enjoyed making play houses under shade trees. Of course, mud pies were stirred up in fruit jar tops. There was a type of clay (grey in color) *[that]* Grandma Alice Edwards showed us on *[the]* side of *[the]* hill near house that had an edible taste. We tasted this smooth sticky clay only once.

May 4 –

I was never bitten by a dog because once he growled and showed his teeth, I had this notice to hike. I have been chased a few times and almost caught at the heels. We lived in rural area, and people kept their bad dogs tied up; otherwise, had a way of shooting bad dogs.

May 5 – Special Gift from Mother

Only my sister Marie made very pretty dresses for Coila and I. Our mother Lucy (Craig) Edwards passed when I was 2 years old. Coila was 4 years old. Marie said mother Lucy sewed beautiful clothes for our family and community. Our gifts were pretty dresses that Marie made for us girls.

May 6 – A Favorite Memory of My Mother

She was a very good seamstress. She made conveniences around our house I was told; like smart housekeepers, convenient shelves and cabinets, etc. I was told that she was creative. One of mother Lucy's legacies for me is craft. (See Appendix D – Mother's Prayer)

May 7 – Advice Given Me

Most of my advice came from Grandma, cousin Sicily Jones, cousin Ella Wade, and other helpful friends and relatives. I also received advice from my sisters, Irene, Marie, and Alice.

May 8 – My Family Mother's Day Tradition

Anna Jarvis of Philadelphia began an effort to establish a nation-wide observance of Mother's Day. She chose the second Sunday in May (May 10, 1908). The 1914 Mother's Day received national recognition. I was born 3 years later – 1917. In rural communities during my childhood, many special occasions were not recognized. Christmas, Easter, and Thanksgiving were highlight occasions for all families. However, May 8th (Mother's Day) became a more noticeable occasion in the late 20's and 30's like other new occasions of today.

May 9 – Childhood Songs and Rhymes
Song:
>Here we go down the new cut road
>And a coop full of chickens makes a heavy load.

Verses:
>I don't like it, I ain't going to take it.
>Here is my collar and I dare you to shake it.

• • •

>The rain is raining all around, it rains on fields and trees
>It rains on the umbrellas here, and on the ships at seas.

• • •

Here we go around the Mulberry Bush, the Mulberry Bush, the Mulberry Bush (repeat 3 times)
So early in the morning.

May 10 – Some Hit Songs

I've got the blues in the bottle and the stopper in my hand[6]

Come with me Where Moonbeams light Tahitian Skies

Last night and night before twenty-four robbers at my door (I went outside, I turned around) to do my best, I stepped right in a hornet's nest[7]

Who stole the lock? I don't know who stole the lock from the hen house door[8]

May 11 – Our Favorite Singing Group or Band

When we had our Pleasant Green Church Revival on 1st Sunday in August, *[it was]* a real home coming for relatives. We invited

---

6 These are lyrics from a Blues song entitled Stingaree Blues, which was recorded by Alberta Hunter, an American Jazz Singer and Songwriter (April 1, 1895 – October 17, 1984)

7 These are lyrics from a jazz song entitled Twenty-Four Robbers; which was recorded by Thomas Wright "Fats" Waller, an American Jazz Pianist and Composer (May 21, 1904 – December 15, 1943)

8 These lyrics can be traced back to a song entitled Who Broke the Lock (on the Henhouse Door). Songwriter is unknown but the lyrics can be traced back to 1893. There are numerous versions on the lyrics.

preachers like Rev*[erend]* Timothy Chambers of Arkansas Baptist Church. He had a quartet of ladies that could sing so beautiful and harmoniously that people would fill our church *[seating]* and *[then]* stand against the walls. Pleasant Green *[Baptist Church]* members named Reverend Chambers, "God's Bandwagon Preacher."

May 12

Ella Fitzgerald – "A-Tisket, A-Tasket; I lost my yellow basket."[9] Ella was a famous singer of the 1939s and 1940s. She had a band that traveled with her *[everywhere]*. She sang while entertaining at many dance events and socials. I was able to see and hear her in person during a social event at Oklahoma City's Civic Auditorium in *[the]* 1940s. She wore a yellow dress.

May 13 – Youth Dancing

We did the Charleston, twisting both feet in and out, one did not need a partner. The Banana Bunch[10] was not too popular. The

---

9 The jazz song A-Tisket, A-Tasket, co-written by Ella Fitzgerald and Al Feldman (later known as Van Alexander), was a major hit in 1938 and became one of the biggest selling records in the 1940s. The actual lyrical phrase where a basket is mentioned in the jazz song A-Tisket, A-Tasket would have actually been *A green and yellow basket, She took my yellow basket, or Just a little yellow basket.* However, some variants of the nursery rhyme that is sung by children in a rhyming game use the phrase *"I lost my yellow basket."*

10 This may not have been too popular because of the association with Josephine Baker's Banana Dance, which became associated with the advertisement of colonial products (i.e., rum, tobacco). Advertisements used images of black females wearing scanty attire similar to Baker's famous banana costume (Henderson, M. G. & Regester, C. B. (2017). The Josephine Baker critical reader: Selected writings on the entertainer and activist. Jefferson, North Carolina: McFarland & Company, Inc., Publishers)

Two Step dance needed a partner. We did Waltz dancing during school events and at parties.

May 14
As a post grad at Douglas High School in Oklahoma City, my sister Irene let me go to Ella Fitzgerald entertainment at Oklahoma City Civic Auditorium. I felt lost, but I did enjoy the concert and of course I learned.

May 15 – High School Prom
This event was one that I never enjoyed.

Our mother Mary Lucy's Uncle Ned E. Williams High School or Gregg County Training School . . . well . . . Graduation in our beautiful white dresses, *[and]* boys in dark suits [with] white shirts [and] black ties were the entertainment for school closing.

May 16 – Military Experience of Someone in Our Family
Uncle Leander Evans, *[the]* first husband *[of]* Aunt Sarah, mother Lucy's sister. Uncle Leander passed before I was old enough to know him. However, we enjoyed looking at his steel hat and brown uniform at Aunt Sarah's house in Longview City. When we visited Aunt Sarah, Coila and I would tip out to her service porch to gaze at Uncle Leander's Army uniform that was mounted on a tall stately stand; a World War I memory.

May 17 – Memory of War During My Childhood

Maybe gentlemen with large young families had some exemption from World War I. Our father Bob did not go to war. I was born February 26, 1917. World War I started in 1914 in European countries between Austria, Hungary, and Serbia in 1914. Woodrow Wilson was president of U.S. The war lasted until 1918. I was about one year old [when] armistice (truce) was signed. Step mom Dora Edwards told us of her memories. She recalled the time as a teen that people were preaching in the streets and praying for peace – "The Word of God is Sweet, Sweet, Sweeter than honey".

**Myrtle Edwards
21 years old in 1938**

May 18 – Continued War Memories (same as May 17)

We always repeated what step mom Dora Edwards told us about the street preaching and praying. During World War I my father was helping to care for 7 children.

May 19 – 1938

Just another photo; 21 years old. Not many childhood photos were made. However, our house with childhood memories burned in 1949. No one took time to photograph us as children. I am glad to find this one of me. – Willie Myrtle Edwards – see September 11th for 7-year-old photo of me.

May 20 – Traditional Graduation Exercises

Some big city schools may have had caps and gowns. Beautiful lace trimmed white dresses were worn during our graduation ceremonies. Male grads wore black suits. Valedictorian student was given chance to deliver farewell speech for the class. The same tune for class grads *[who]* march *[is]* still used today; however, with more sophistication, maybe. Earlier schools had only piano music, especially in our area. We had salutatory (opening) and valedictory (farewell) by best student.

May 21 – Year of My Graduation

I graduated from Greenville High School in 1935 *[located in]* suburb of Longview, Texas. Now that our outstanding in-law, Uncle Ned Williams, was so well thought of . . . the community decided that this educational facility should be remembered as N.E. Williams High School. I was not able to go to college in Texas. Papa let me move to Aunt Sarah (Craig) Bailey*['s, in Oklahoma]*. I enrolled in Douglas High School as a past graduate to take more science classes and home economy. During summer of 1935 and 1936, I worked with Sister Irene (my hero) and saved my money for Langston University.

May 22 – Number of Students *[at]* Douglas High School, Senior Class

There were about 18 students in my senior class at N. E. Williams High.[11] In my post graduate class of Oklahoma City's Douglas

---

11 Originally named Greenville High School when W. Myrtle Edwards attended.

THE START OF SUMMER

[High School] there were 100 students. I had the opportunity to learn more with extra-curricular subjects and many new experiences in Douglas High that I can appreciate now.

May 23 –
In Texas, my first high school class attendance *[size]* was about 150 or 180 [students]. Elementary and high *[school were]* on same grounds. *[These schools served]* two communities, Greenville and Pleasant Green. We attended Pleasant Green Elementary and after graduation from 6th grade – on to Greenville High to enter 7th grade. Yes, we walked three miles while Elderville High School[12] bus drove by us *[while we]* walked in rain or shine.

May 24 – Did I have Homework?
Yes, we always had homework; especially math and English. We had used textbooks (used White hand-me-downs). Some of these books were too advanced for the grades in which we were placed. However, I would like to have the now famous Blue Book Speller and McGuffey Reader in my possession. These books are collectors' items.

May 25 – Age 12 Years, Some Proud Moments
I was very proud when I learned how to use my mother Lucy's sewing machine. She was said to be a very good seamstress. I remember that I had to hide to make a blue print dress

---

12 Elderville High School was the segregated high school that was only for white people.

because Coila was tattling to Papa that I was messing up some material – "Thanks" – Papa gave her no attention. In 1970 I made sister Coila a fur coat. What goes around comes around. It took her 50 years to understand my childhood wishes.

May 26 – Memorial Day Tradition

We had May 1st as Memorial Day tradition. We traveled about 5 or 6 miles to our community cemetery. All of our community joined in burial décor with live plants and flowers. My grandfather Clayborne Edwards' cousin Grant Harper and my father were the main directors for cleaning and decoration of the grounds.

This day was edged with a huge picnic. After the picnic we picked up trash from the forest edges and we all wagoned to our homes. There (maybe) were a few cars.

May 27 – Grable Cemetery

Everyone who did not bring hoe or shovel, raked *[and]* shared with someone for cutting *[the]* grass. Hatchets were necessary for some tough bushes. This cemetery was fenced next to a goat pasture. Sometimes the goats broke through the fence and ate flower decorations and plants. [A] White gardener *[named]* Mitchell received many complaints about his goats in our Grable Cemetery.

May 28 – 1938 [to] 41, My musical instrumentation

I started with piano practice for an extra activity in college studies *[but]* became too board [sic] and I did not like going next door to practice piano. Home Economy studies were enough. I regret that I did not make a special time to continue piano practice.

Memory Class Credits[13]

Give memory credits to Wilton Stewart, you should
My visit to memory class was good.

With Freelance Teacher we learned well
He placed forget and memory in adjustment cell.

A primary class seemed too strange,
Yet Freelance Teacher covered a wide range.

We all enjoyed his memory expertise
With special pointing, he aimed to please.

From class we started with thankful hearts,
With one day's training, we were to start.

One day I yelled, where are my keys
With memory practice, I found them with ease.

I like to share these memory thoughts,
So, people can realize the value he taught.

---

13 See Appendix E – Reflections from Myrtle Stewart for inspiration behind this poem.

May 29 – My Closest Friend During Childhood

My cousin was a close friend. Naomi Harper, cousin Malinda (Wade) Harper's daughter. The Harper and Edwards family were very close. Cousin Grant and cousin Malinda Harper's youngest son, Doctor Robert Lee Harper, is a dentist in Longview, Texas. His address *[is]* 1005 S. M.L. King Blvd., Longview, Texas, 75602. Phone 903-753-2716.

May 30 – Myrtle's Curiosity, One Antique Kept from Childhood (1926-27)

Our loving grandmother Alice (Wade) Edwards knew me very well! When I was about 10 years old, I always watched my grand mom go to her vegetable garden to pick vegetables; so, I could slip in*[to]* her bedroom and open her trunk to quickly open and fan with a small ribbon laced gutta-percha[14] fan. Gutta-percha is a rubber sap from tropical trees that is refined into a plastic like solid. I do not know how she knew about my "sneak," but before she passed, she told her granddaughter (cousin Nicey Price) to be sure to give Myrtle the gutta-percha fan. I still have Ma Edwards' fan. I am sure that it is over 100 years old. Gutta-percha = a rubbery substance derived from the latex of tropical trees (like plastic).

---

14 A tough natural plastic substance produced from the sap of several Malaysian or Brazilian trees. It resembles rubber, but contains more resin. It was used in the construction of Victorian style hand fans, hair combs, and jewelry. The substance is also used as a filling for root canals.

May 31 – Good Bath-Time Stories

We heated water to fill a large aluminum wash tub. We packed water from a spring that ran into a deepened rock bed. This water was purer than city water. The distance of the water spring from our house was about 65 yards (1/4 mile). We always had a water well that ran dry. There was not much to do in our daily program. On this uphill *[track]* through some forestry, there were things to enjoy like eating Black Balls *[i.e., Black Walnuts]*, and small tree berries. There *[were]* many beautiful trees here also. There were chinky pen *[also known as Chinkapin or Chinquapin]* trees in this hillside area above our spring.

MONTH OF MARRIAGE AND WELL-BEING

June 1 – A Strange Person Lived in Our Town

There was a hermit in our town; his name was Rufus Woods. He also liked living in the woods. He stole chickens and vegetables from our community. He acted with respect around our father. Rufus had a horse that he rode from the forest where *[he fried]* chickens. When our father Robert Edwards was funeralized, he stood very close to our church steps to meet the family. He finally moved into a little cabin near dad's house. He always made his moves around late at night or very early mornings.

June 2 – The Funniest Nicknames in Our Town (Longview, Texas)

- Lap Wade – Curtis Wade (cousin)
- Duok Portly – Henry Portley (cousin)
- Bud Allen – White friend of family
- Rock – father Robert Edwards
- Boo Harper – Daisey Harper (cousin)
- Honey – Mother Lucy Edwards

June 3 – Sleeping Under the Stars (in Gregg County)

Our father was a cotton, corn, and vegetable farmer. After cotton was picked from the boll, and filled a deep-sided planked wagon, evening was the time to take it to the Cotton Gin. We always hopped in the wagon of cotton and counted shooting stars for at least 3 miles to the gin *[in]* late evenings. We counted stars and made wishes that we would meet a very nice young man to marry. This made us "sleepless."

June 4 – 16 Miles from Oklahoma City, Dunjee High School *[in]* Choctaw, Okla.

Cook out with leader Myrtle Stewart with Girl Scout Troup from Dunjee High School. I was a fifth-grade teacher during this time. We spent one Saturday afternoon in a big woodsy park cooking. There were only about 6 of us. We wore our green uniforms. I was assistant Home Economy teacher at Dunjee High.

June 5 – Our Styled Campout

Texas Freedom Day[15] was June 19. Big sun umbrellas *[were]* necessary all day for celebration. Our country life style was one that gave us a chance to enjoy sleeping and playing especially

---

15 Also known as Juneteenth Independence Day, an American holiday that commemorates the June 19, 1865 announcement of the abolition of slavery in the state of Texas. Although the Emancipation of slaves in the United States was officially declared effective on January 1, 1863, Texas was not a battleground; so, the news of emancipation did not reach Texas until Major General Gordon Granger landed in Galveston, Texas with the news on June 19th, 1865.

in summer time. It was fun to make playhouses under the large dense forest trees. . . with protection from sun and rain. *[However,]* no real camp outs were experienced. On 19th of June most people traveled to Easton, Texas (Village of Black America) for all day sports and eat out. Most people had cars at this time.

June 6 – Who Went on Sniper Hunts? (About 1930)

I have been on a different kind of hunt. My grandfather Clayborne Edwards had a love for Wild Bee collecting for honey. Pa Edwards had about 10 Bee hives in his fruit orchard. Relatives and friends with flash lights and lanterns joined the bee hunt collecting party. At evening time bees were found clinging to twigs on tree limbs. Pails of water were "fetched" for wetting down the wings. Bees could not fly *[with wet wings]*. These twigs of wet Bees were bagged for a beehive box in pa's fruit orchard. Everyone was covered for protection. They were afraid to get close to Pa or Myrtle – real bee robbers.

June 7 – What I Learned to Cook as a Youth (the 1930s)

My step mother Dora Edwards of whom we called Mrs. Dora, as I did not learn to call anyone mother. I wanted to cook but had not [sic] chance even as a teenager. For some reason she said we were wasteful. I was allowed to make biscuits once. Papa did not know who *[made the biscuits but]* he liked my biscuits. So, I did not get a chance to make biscuits anymore. I learned how to cook Spanish rice while working in Oklahoma City for my college friends. I was a late bloomer for cooking.

June 8 – Horse Riding

Papa had a pretty red horse named Mary. We enjoyed riding her to nearby creek for water. We would lead Mary to our large "L" porch to straddle her, using only a blanket on her back. We loved *[to]* pet *[our]* horse *[called]* Mary. I think Coila learned how to (plat) braid hair while practicing on Mary's pretty bushy tail.

Longview, Texas: My First Job (1929 – 32)

We Edwards children, as farmers daughters had many little part-time jobs that were for the most part seasonal; like helping those who ask us to help weed their crops of corn or cotton with hand hoes. These were 8-hour jobs and at that time we had no other choice. This was a time when crops had to be gathered either for our home use or either we could work for pay.

June 10 – Jobs, How Much Did We get Paid? (1929 – 30)

Everything was very reasonable to buy. So, since cost, supply and demand work together for our economy, a day's work *[was]* $1.00, 1.50, or 2.00 per day. Growth and technology also have had much to do with job pay, as well as some other factors *[in]* this day in time. In our community there was a huckster man. *[The man's]* name, Huckster Ed Mears. In other words, a peddler who collects community products for sale in cities. So, Coila and I gave Mr. Ed Mears some peas to sell for us. Transportation was 20 cents on the dollar. So, if Ed Mears sold our vegetables for $1.00, we earned 80 cents. No, Papa had so many vegetables until he did not miss them.

June 11 – Other Paying Jobs (1937 – 38)

When I was in Douglas High in Oklahoma my brother-in-law, Sam Walker, found a ragged old sewing machine and brought it to his house for me to repair. I had a fix-it spirit. Although it had no bobbin case, somehow, I made it work for me. I was over joyed that neighbors chose me to make their children's' school attire. I have always had in my mind "find a way or make it."

June 12 – Chased by an Animal

Yes, I was once chased by a dog. *[But, more notably,]* we had a big black mean mule named Mag. When we teased her, she would try to bite us; we always ran from her.

June 13 – Were You Ever in a Parade?

No, but *[I]* enjoyed traveling to Marshall, Texas, about 40 miles from Longview to see the college students parade before the football game with Wiley and Bishop College. I was about 8 years old and I remember some to the parading students yelling "Sting them Hornets." This must have been Bishop's slogan because Wiley College boasted as "Wiley Wild Cats." My sister Marie spent one year as a student at Wiley College.

June 14 – Other Parade Memories (1938)

Douglas High School Marching Band and Pep squad *[was renown as a spirited marching band]*. When Douglas High school football team played a visiting team like Tulsa, Muskogee, or Okmulgee High School, the band and pep squad, under the direction of music director Zelia N. Breaux was very competitive. Douglas High band was a winning band and on many occasions was highly appreciated by Oklahoma City downtown merchants.

June 15 – Childhood Memories about a Death

I was thirteen years old when brother Rogers Edwards (3rd oldest after sister Irene) became injured and was unconscious. He was lifeless for three days and never recovered. He had been to a church conference. Rogers was driving, cousin Paul and Reginald Hutchings *[who were passengers in the vehicle]* were slightly injured when Rogers traveled over a wooden bridge and turned over. That was in 1930. Today's technology (with life support) may have made a difference.

June 16 – My Happiest Memory as a Youth (1928)

When my father Bob "Rock" Edwards bought a new 1928 Ford, the styles had changed and the body style looked more like a Chevrolet. We could hear our cousin Grant Harper talking loud from one hill to the other hills. He says, "Rock bought a brand-new Ford car today – He gave $400 cash dollars for it." I was 11 years old.

June 17 – How About Swimming?

I still have not tried to swim. I feel like Summer 1998 will be my chance. *[When I was growing-up in Texas]* there was a big creek of water near our home, but we were afraid to try the water. I am like the person who wrote "I believe I can fly." I started to drive a car again after 45 years away from the wheel.[16]

June 18
We did not go swimming. However, there were White boys who would drive from Longview City to the beautiful blue water swimming holes. We mischievously thought about filling the sandy banks beside the swim holes with sticking grass burs. It is true that some kids did this.

June 19 – A Favorite Memory of Father and Freedom Day
Our papa always bought good clothes for us. Sister Marie Edwards made our pretty dresses from the nice material or fabrics. On June 19th most Texas people took this date for a holiday.[17] Emancipation Proclamation issued by President Abraham Lincoln, effective January 1, 1863, freed all slaves; *[however,]* the news for freedom *[of slaves in Texas]* came later and recorded on June 19th.

June 20 – Father's Advice
Our father was cautious about our table manners. I remember how papa taught us to use a fork. [Also,] we were never allowed

---

16 Myrtle stopped driving at the age of 34 in 1951, seven years after marrying Richard Stewart. She did not get behind the wheel of an automobile again until 1996 at the age of 79.

17 See May 22 and Footnote 11. I learned more about my history at Douglas High School than at Greenville High. I had the opportunity to learn more with extra-curricular subjects and many new experiences in Douglas High that I can appreciate now.

getting into anyone's car except our relatives. He says "always put a handle to adult names, like hello Mr. Jones, Hello Mrs. Smith. Further, yes sir and yes mam is southern, but it demands a certain kind of respect. This is the way we had to express ourselves.

June 21 – A Special Gift from Father (Texas and California)

Papa gave me an expensive glass point fountain pen when I was in high school. When papa visited me in Los Angeles (about 1951) he said "let's go downtown. I want to buy you a gift for remembrance." Papa bought me a set of willow decorated dishes.

June 22 – Rural Pleasant Green Community

Our special nature place for us was about 10 yards from our house and sometimes down the hill. There was cool spring water running out of hill rocks. No pollution near*[by]*. *[Of course, it is noted that]* our yard well ran dry often. This water spring was surrounded with beautiful Dogwood trees and Huckleberry trees *[from]* which we ate the berries, Black Ball Berry trees, and Blackberry vines that we could rock the snakes out of. We had loads of fun decorating our hats with flowers, wild roses, violets, wild daises, and pretty ferns.

June 23 – Skinny Dipping

Caucasian boys came to a large blue lake at times, not too far from our home to swim. We do not know if they skinny dipped. If they did skinny dip and roll on the lake shore sand, our mischievous neighbors saw to it that their bodies met all grass burs that they kept mixed in the sand. There was another "Blue Hole Lake" that town kids liked visiting that was in an adjoining community.

June 24 – We Liked Making "Mud Pies"

[We had fun] making mud pies in our play houses under our many stately gum trees where we kept that gum tree trunk hacked to start a sweet gum drip. We chewed this gum while we filled jar tops with mud pies in our play houses.

June 25 – Barefoot Summer Fun

Yes, we had good shoes, but a few moments within hot summer days, *[we enjoyed the opportunity]* to free our feet and enjoy cool wet dirt or mud; *[it]* was a "cool specialty." We pulled off our shoes many times to cross a shallow creek, but *[wear our shoes when we]* see our house and ma Edwards' home. We had to watch how we walked through a trail of weeds; there were pin point sized red bugs that would bite legs just enough to make you itch. *[Yes,]* wading in water and washing legs was often.

June 26 – My Experience Stepping on Something

Yes, I remember stepping on something slick and wiggling. . . I was too afraid to check out the shallow water. My move was hasty. When summer came the sand and dirt usually became very hot; you wore shoes for burs and other protection. I probably have stepped on a small fish or frog.

June 27 – Talk About a Bike

No bike. We had to foot it everywhere. In this country life we had an opportunity to appreciate and enjoy nature. Our mode of moving faster than walking was by wagon, which also is not too fast.

June 28 – I learned to Sew as a Youth

We had a treadle foot machine.[18] We did all kinds of needle work. Sewing has always been my best hobby. This sewing has been good therapy for me.

June 29 – Making Swings

Near the front yard of our home, I remember a long rope looped across a heavy tree limb *[that hung down]* about 2 feet from *[the]* ground *[with]* a 14 or 15-inch-long board that was "V" notched at each end to anchor rope. Here we enjoyed bracing our feet against the ground and pumping away to help lift oneself and swing into the air. Sometimes someone would give us a quick pull backwards for help. Away up in the air was fun, but when you pump strongly against the ground until someone says "I'm going to tell you are swinging too high." Then it is fun time to "let the cat die" by holding side ropes tightly, bending over, letting feet slightly drag ground while slowly stopping. . . this was fun.

---

18 This was probably a Singer Treadle Sewing Machine with a decorative cast iron base foot pedal.

June 30 – Something That I thought was Very Beautiful

Our grand-ma Alice Edwards' yard was very beautiful. She had Dogwood bushes, Bridal Wreath bushes, Pink Easter bushes. I always broke a long switch of her bridal wreath bush and anchored it around my head. She had touch-me-not flowers, zinnia*[s]*, and lilies of all kind. She had John Quill and a hugh mound of vines *[that]* were very dense and about 5 ½ feet across with tiny yellow blossoms. This plant was strong enough to hold us up when we chanced to run across just to tease the wasp and bees. Because we were rural children, we knew how. Yes, we were stung a few times. . .we did not stop. No – we found time to knock down wasp's nest and run. Daring episodes, huh?

VACATION TIME

July 1 – Outside Games Made up
1. Hide and go seek. Four or five people hide behind house tree or shed house while person number six would close their eyes and sing a song. Everyone runs to hide out. *[After number six finishes singing a song,]* all *[need to]* hide, yell is made. If no one answers it is time to look for each person. Home station had to be touched before caught to be a winner. Sometimes this was called post office.
2. "Skip-to -my-Lou, skip-to -my-Lou, skip-to -my-Lou my darling."[19] *[You will]* see a group of girls skipping with hardly no end to skipping. The skipping was judged of course.

July 2 – An Inside Game We Made Up
Mississippi was printed in many places in our geography. While turning pages very fast, each geography word player who could

---

19 This song can be traced back to the 1840s. It is a simple game of stealing or swapping partners while dancing in a circle and in square dancing.

find Mississippi state first would yell "Mississippi" and make one mark for themselves. This game lasted as long as this word could be found by word players. The most fun came after the game was finished. {We would sing] M-I crooked letter crooked letter I crooked letter crooked letter I humpback humpback I.

July 3 – Fire Works
My father bought the kind of fireworks that you throw on pavement and rub like you are dancing with your feet to make popping noise. We also had a few fire crackers and sparklers.

July 4 – Independence Day Tradition
Very little excitement was witnessed for July 4th. We may have cooked a fancy meal. I remember how we found mounds of small balls of dirt heaped in piles. We found fun in digging up these dirt mounds for fish bait worms. So, going fishing was one of the July 4th activities. Earth worms was a must for good fishing bate.

July 5 – Another July Remembrance
I remember visiting our mother Lucy's favorite cousin Sicily and David Jones. They always had a lot of food, especially watermelon, chicken, etc. I remember papa taking us on fishing trip to the Sabine River near the beautiful clear lake that stayed blue. The communities big cotton gin was in background water ways. This gin was owned by White man Gardner Mitchell who *[was]* a friend to Black people.

July 6 – Carnival Fun

Papa took us to see Barnum and Bailey circus in Longview, Texas, 8 miles from home in a wagon. This was first time eating cotton candy, flavored ice crystals, and shaved ice cups.

– School Fun

In spring time four schools enjoyed amusement in Greenville High School Park; Longview South Side High, Greenville High, Freedom High, and Pleasant Green Elementary. These schools had educational contests indoors and outdoor sports. There were many concessions stands and patrons with food baskets.

July 7 – What Kind of Games and Rides?

When we attended Dallas, Texas State Fair, I remember riding on [the] Ferris wheel. All rides were less than $1.00. Other games and rides featured electric car rides, caterpillar rides, Notch pole hammering, horse shoes, polo rides, etc. Our sister Marie Johnson and husband Obie Johnson had made their home in Dallas.

July 8 – State Fair and County Fair

I remember Gregg County Fair in Longview where mother Alice Edwards always had beautiful award-winning quilts. I remember two first prize quilts. The "Star Quilt" made of very small ½ inch stars. She also made a wedding ring quilt. She had fancy fruit canning prizes also.

July 9 – Going to a Circus

Our Aunt Sarah Bailey lived at 2508 N. E. 13th Street in Oklahoma City, Oklahoma. My father sent me to Oklahoma to live with her and further my education. I was pleased. Aunt Sarah lived across the street from the fair ground and recreation park. We watched Barnum and Bailey move in with their animals in cages. *[It was an experience]* seeing the large elephants pass by. We could see a lot very early every day. I could see Cherokee Indians dance in tribal costumes. There are more Indians in Oklahoma than any other state except Arizona.

July 10 – Summertime Memories

Our summertime activities became fun as we played with our cousin Ella Wade's girls; Sophia and Jennie Wade. They were our neighbors about 1 ½ blocks away. We always ran to pass Aunt Harriet and Aunt Amanda Pierce's house, because they were bossy and nosey. Our games with Sophia and Jennie Wade were singing

>Go-in and Out the Window,
>Go-in and Out the Window,
>Go-in and Out the Window.[20]

---

20 The lyrics trace back to the 19th Century in American history. Subsequently, A song composed by Lew Pollack became popular as a children's music standard around 1911.

We also sang

>Hold up the gate high as the sky
>And let king George's horses by.[21]

Singing and marching *[was a favorite pastime]*. *[Playing]* "Hop Scotch" also was a must.

July 11 – Childhood Fishing
I enjoyed fishing. We liked watching cousin Annie Wade fish. She was always lucky to catch a dozen or more each fishing trip. This cousin was grandma Alice Wade Edwards' nephew's wife. The nephew's name was Lonnie Wade.

July 12 – Fishing
I remember catching some small cat fish. Fishing was like a game to us. At times when we had a bad fish day and needed fish to bite our hooks, we sanded[22] the creek (or used a net) for small minor fish that swam close to water's edge. Some folk would take hoe or rakes and muddy small ponds of water and fish would float on top of water. This act was against the law – could be fined if caught.

---

21 The origin of these words are unknown; however, King George V "preferred to review his army on horseback, riding high enough to be seen by the ranks on horseback" (Great War Blog, 27 Oct 1915 – Tribal Belt).

22 A process of building a dike or barricade. To fill up with sand to create a harbor or smaller area or body of water.

July 13 – Our Favorite Candy

Our papa thought that large peppermint stick was our favorite candy. This was the first item that we found across our Christmas gift boxes early Christmas morning. The (small salad plate size) peanut patty was another favorite. My father made candy also. He worked for a candy kitchen in Tyler, Texas before he married.

July 14 – My Favorite Snack at Home

Fig trees outlined our backyard near our big bungalow house. Our family made fig preserves often, so my favorite snack was buttered figwich and a glass of milk. However, the best snack for figs was picked from the tree. Our father had many figs for sale in the city of Longview, Texas. Figs have always been an expensive fruit.

July 15 – Going on a Picnic

Our picnics always came on occasions like June 19, when most Black people celebrate freedom from slavery. We, along with other relatives would travel to an all-Black town Village called Eastern, Texas. Many people enjoyed this picnic with sharing baskets of food. Games like sack racing, baseball, and foot racing – and other fun like games.

July 16 – Party Games

Musical chairs; whispering gossip; pinning donkey's tail. Most activities included singing and storytelling especially; especially ghost stories. Some true to life stories also were interesting.

July 17 – Heat Waves

During the month between May and September, we always kept all windows open as long as we were at home. Papa made a large dining room fan about twenty-five inches by twenty-five inches attached to room ceiling. Attached *[to the fan was]* a long rope for us to pull during meal time. When draught [sic] or heat wave made crops perish, most times farmers had barned up and/or canned all harvest surplus. Sharing and bartering was common for helping neighbors. Although we packed water from a downhill spring, we had to keep enough for our chickens.

July 18 – Trying to Stay Cool

Fanning and drinking water was a must. Sprinkling our heads with water, wading in nearby creeks, *[and]* sometimes even pouring water on our heads. We had many large trees around our house. Trees with many limbs, leaves, and branches tend to make hot air cooler. With dirt roads, unlike paved streets, this coolness was always a God send. Even city people did not know the five cooling systems that people have today. The rurales were cooler.

July 19 – My Favorite Holiday of the Year

Christmas of course; it was fun to look for gifts, candy, and learn new songs and poems. We visited relatives and friends saying "Hello, Christmas give!" The quick speaker was supposed to get a material response from slowest speaker. Most times a smile or small gift was given.[23]

---

23 This "Christmas Give" greeting was apparently practiced between the Edwards relatives in Texas when Myrtle Stewart was an adolescent.

July 20 – Birthday Party Memories

On about three or four country hills our relatives had big bungalow houses. Cousin Wade Jones and wife Matilda and their sons and daughters enjoyed giving big parties. Everyone young and old were invited to eat chicken, cake, and watermelon. Games like (1) musical chairs (i.e., four chairs placed for five people to be seated when music stops and standing person loses), (2) making signs for players to guess their occupation,[24] and (3) Whispering Gossip with eight to ten people repeating same or whispering words to see if last person in line whispers same gossip.

July 21 – My Neatest Shoes

My neatest shoes were black leather roman sandals with straps fastening up the side leg from ankle with pretty buttons.

Black Leather Roman Sandal

July 22 – Power Outage (in Rural Texas)

Kerosene fuel lighting for lamps was popular, so we had no knowledge of power outage. Use of oil lamps for reading, wood stones for cooking and warming our home *[was all that we knew]*. Our rural community now enjoys electrical power. Our big white

---

24 This obviously was an early version on the segment of a game called Pictionary that was invented by Robert Angel in 1985.

brick church, Pleasant Green Baptist, was for many years powered by a Delco system power house for lighting. . . No power outage could happen with this independent power system. This was our power system from the year 1925; as early as I can remember; to 1950.

July 23 – Creek Flood

There was a large creek of water down *[the]* hill from our house. When big rains fell – big creek was wide and muddy. A large tree was bent and growing across this creek. I remember times when creek was not water swelled from bank to bank. We would at times walk the trunk of the tree and leap to the bank on the other side. *[Of course,]* this was too dangerous when deep and muddy.

July 24 – Tornados, Hurricanes, and High Winds (Oklahoma City)

In 1946 Richard Stewart and I lived at 2508 N. E. 13th Street, Oklahoma City. This was a newly built neighborhood called Edwards Edition. One morning about 5:00 AM we were awakened by the whine of ambulances speeding on *[a]* nearby highway in route to hospitals. The radio news revealed that many cyclone victims were stricken during early hours in a town south of Oklahoma City. This seemed like a nightmare. A few years later a cyclone struck a mid-west *[part of the]* city; an objectional area for certain races to live in Oklahoma City.

July 25 – Thunder and Lightening

I was afraid of thunder and lightning as a child. And when I was about 13 years old, step mom Dora said "Myrtle, when God gets ready to take you away, fear will not help, so just pray for strength."

July 26 – Special Boat Memories (L.A., California)

During vacation time from civil service (Post Office) job in February 1977. I took a trip on Sun Princess ship to Caracas, Venezuela, South America. My friends would not join me, so I had to travel alone. I made friends. My cabin dweller from Ohio was not friendly, but she was okay. Our first flight stop *[in-route to the ship]* was New Orleans, Louisiana. *[Then,]* we flew to Puerto Rico to board *[the]* ship. In one week's time, we sailed by and anchored on five of the many Virgin Islands. The last two islands were Trinidad and Tobago. My ship table guests were funny when they excited me to look away from my plate so they could place a spoon of escargot on my plate. I ate all around this spoon full *[of escargot]*. Although Escargot (snails) is a French delicacy, I knew that I did not order something in a shell. They smiled this joke away *[during]* this ten-day cruise.

[While on cruise] I visited Caracas, Venezuela. This country is supposed to be the most up-to-date of countries in Latin America. About one out of ten persons is supposed to be Negro. Venezuela calls itself a republic.

July 27 – A Family Vacation Trip (Henderson, Texas)

We visited cousin Ella Burnett and family every August during their church revival. This seemed quality time for us because cousin and other distant cousins were so nice – the Durgees and the Piques; they all looked like Caucasian people. Henderson, Texas was about 30 miles from our home in Longview, Texas.

July 28 – Another Vacation: World's Fair [sic] in Vancouver, Canada (1986)

Canada experience – "The Best." Daughter, Marquetta Brown and sons; Jerami, Javier, and Jahrod Matlock; took me to World's Fair 1986 in Canada.

July 30 – River, Lake, Beach Memories

Yes, we went on River banks, not beaches. Papa always tried fishing on special days. Sister Coila and I played on edge of water. I remember swinging on limbs of trees over the water of Sabine River and Clear Lake. These water ways we crossed over when we had opportunity to follow our family to Longview City in our wagon of course. These water ways were attracted by tourist [sic].

July 31 – Bus Ride Experience

In early years, no bus rides, no train rides, or airplane trips. No, my first bus ride was from Longview, Texas to Oklahoma City when papa sent me to live with my aunt Sarah (Craig) Bailey and later sister Irene Walker.

HARVEST TIME

August 1 – Another Memory, The Wagon Ride
The humming, the singing, game playing while bumping along is always in my memory. We played games; Colia and I found time to face each other while riding, slapping our hands together. Doing a double hand slap and repeating a poem in unison. "Peach porridge hot, Peach porridge cold, Peach porridge in the pot nine days old.[25]" *[We would site those words]* over and over.

August 2 – My Childhood Home
Our father Robert Edwards built a large bungalow house about ¼ mile from our grandparents, who lived on the next hill. Our house had kitchen, dining room, three bedrooms, with a fourth skeleton like room started (never finished) on back of the third bedroom. We had a very large hallway between kitchen, dining room, and living room that extended to a small back porch. The front of our house had a huge L shaped porch. I was a baby when this building was constructed.

---

25 This is an old English nursery rhyme that can be found with other Mother Goose children's rhymes, dating back to the 1700s.

Our home was in the center of beautiful forestry of pink and red bud trees, Dog Wood trees of white blossoms, nut trees, Plum trees, and we enjoyed the setting.

August 3 – Good Advice
"Do your best and worry not. Fretting never solves problems. Worry puts fuzzing in your head, a knot in your stomach, and a pack on your back. Nothing is as helpful as concern. Indifference never sees the problem; worry tangles them; but concern unravels them. So, be enterprising enough to do your best and be truthful enough to leave it with God. . . Leroy Brownlow".[26]

August 4 – Climbing Big Hills
There were many big hills in my community with high growing bushes and many sticks, insects of all kinds. Catching a twig or bush to help pull body up hills *[was]* some fun. When sometimes the hills were muddy and the roadways *[up the hill were wet]* our vehicle would slow down a bit. That would give us a chance to

---

26 The words of Leroy Brownlow made an impact on Myrtle when she either heard him speak or read his written word during the 1970s- or 1980s-time frame. Leroy Brownlow; born April 30, 1914; was a Preacher, author, writer, publisher and business man who pastored the Polytechnic Church of Christ in Fort Worth, Texas. Under his leadership the church was a dynamic and aggressive conservative church that provided a positive influence. The church was once the biggest congregations in its denomination. It was the first church in Fort Worth to have air conditioning, off-street parking, and one of the first to be on television. Leroy Brownlow passed on November 8, 2002.

sing "I think I can ♪, I think I can ♪"[27] like the little train engine.

August 5 – Richard Stewart's 62nd Birthday Party

In December 1980 there was a surprise party given for Richard Stewart. He had said "No one can surprise me." His brother Eddie did not know about the party either or he would have told.

August 6 – Childhood Board Games

Tic-Tac-Toe was a game with squares drawn on cardboard tablet backs. Using buttons to *[see who could]* line them *[up]* first as winner of game.

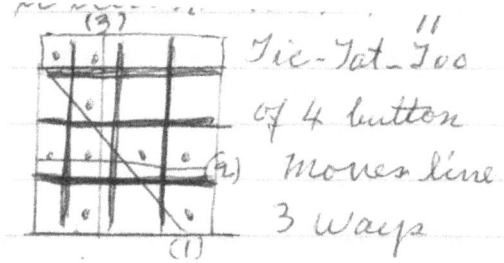

Picture of board using only 2 players

Players could choose one line each out of 4 lines to play. A diagonal line could be discovered within checked off *[squares]* on the board.[28]

We played See-saw with plank or board resting on tree stump or heavy stationary block. We used long board across stump to have seat on each end for See-saw partner. We bounced up and down by pushing feet against ground.

---

27 Plotnick, Roy E. (2012). "In Search of Watty Piper: The History of the 'Little Engine' Story". New Review of Children's Literature and Librarianship.

28 While tic-tac-toe dates back to Ancient Egyptian times and is usually in a 3 X 3 grid, grids of varying sizes have developed, as evidenced here.

We made board bats to play softball. Rags and strings made a good softball; just wrap tightly.

August 7 – Card Games Played at Home
Our papa did not allow us to play card games; so, . . . He Won. I learned how to play Whist card games at Langston University with friends. However, card games were not in my best interest. . . seemingly a waste of my time. I played Whist only to complete a table of four players until relieved by an interested person.

August 8 – Weight Problem
Yes, I was a chubby little girl who at one time after I reached age 14 decided to chew fiber and substances from food, and *[then]* discard remaining chewed food and fiber. Five or six years later my sister Irene was also concerned about my shape and size. She bought me a full-length foundation garment. I appreciated her help. . . And even now. I can realize what change of foundation meant to me.

August 9 – My Best Talent
Public speaking. We stood on boxes very often to hear each other make the best speech in our way of thinking.

When I was in grade school, I thought that I could spell better than my cousin Georgia Mae Borders. We "wrangled" with each other in spelling lines with about eight students who were so capable of staying number one or number two; with six students always below us in spelling line. The best student in line-up was always Myrtle Edwards or Georgia Mae Borders.

August 10 – A Time to Get Lost

I was at Douglas High, 600 North High in Oklahoma City during the Fall semester; my first post-graduate year. My uncle George Bailey dropped me off at school every morning. *[Then,]* I had to *[walk]* eight blocks back to 613 North Eastern. *[One day]* I came out a different door for home with aunt Sarah Bailey. This made a difference. After a few moments I could see that I was near downtown Oklahoma City; so, I quickly checked my direction daily.

August 11 – Playing in Sprinkler or Hose

1. Our water games were wading in shallow creek water and trying to catch small minnow fish to use as fish bate on our hooks. We had fun. . . .
2. Rural families had no sprinkler system, so you see from first story that we had more than enough water to splash *[at the creek]*

August 12 – Talking About Wasp and Bees

We thought that wasp nest*[s]* under the eaves of our house were one of nature's natural forms of art for us to knock down with a reed cane fishing pole to decorate our woodside play house. You can realize that sometimes we did not get away with this act fast enough before getting stung. A little turpentine or camphor oil was applied to the sting. However, I learned to keep my distance with a good run.

August 13 – Family Song
While riding with the family or when we wanted to hold a revival near our play house across the dusty road from our house, Coila and I would sing a song. The songs we tried to sang -- Down by the Riverside Going to Lay Down My Burden; Ain't Going to Study War No More; Oh, Mary Don't You Weep; and Love Lifted Me. Naturally, *[we would also conduct]* our church school teachings.

August 14 – Our Bedroom
Papa Bob was a carpenter. He built a large bungalow house with six rooms, a wide hall about six- and one-half feet wide, divided the bedrooms from living room, dining *[room]*, and kitchen. The large "L" shaped porch was huge also. Our bedrooms were next to the "L" shaped porch.

August 15 – Overnight Stay with Friends
Overnight staying was only with relatives. Grandmother Alice's house *[was]* first in my memory. When I was about 13 years old, I spent one Christmas overnight at ma Alice's house. She had to secretly put out Santa's gifts for me. She had to pass through my guest room with my gifts. I am sure that she knew or realized that I would not sleep, and knew that I would peep.

August 16 – About Running Away from Home
When our father married Dora Jamison, we felt that our sole help *[and attention from papa]* had been greatly divided because his new wife had three children. *[Dora's children were]* a year or

two younger than us. Papa saw our displeasures. *[He]* figured that we had run away plans. After papa talked to us about some other girls' bad experiences *[about running away,]* we forgot our plans.

August 18 – Roller Skaters

Sometimes when it rained in our rural community, we found fun in scooting around in the mud. We had no place to skate. Different shapes were made with our toes in doodling in the mud. This was fun. Making our own hours of fun with what nature offered was natural to rural children. Stick horses from broom sticks was fun also.

August 19 – Experiencing Home Sickness (1930 to 1944)

I had no chance to experience home sickness while trying to discover a new area for advancement. While being ambitious, I always tried to learn something new with every new location. *[From]* Longview, Texas to Oklahoma City, *[and]* Langston University to Los Angeles, Ca; Success is a journey, not a destination.

August 20 – My First Taste of Pop or Soda

Grandfather Clayborne Edwards had a little grocery store and gas station. He also had a vegetable cannery next door to his store. This is a place where I tasted soda pop *[for the]* first time. Pa Edwards sold gasoline at 9 cents per gallon *[and]* pop had a better taste then, than today.

August 21 – Early Experience with Make-Up

Facial powder was the only *[store bought]* make-up I can remember at our house *[when I was a little girl]*. A good hairdo with straightening comb *[would frustrate me]* and I was tired of being burned as a child. I am glad *[to now have]* hair conditioning. My hair needed no hot comb. *[My sister Cootsy and I created our own make-up and hairdo.]* Wild flowers weighed down our hats for fun. It was fun to take the phosphorus lighted tails of poor little fire flies that slowly flew around with a twinkle. Their little torn rear-ends (match head size) looked like diamonds on our ears. Just *[the two of us]* about 8 to 10 years old. *[See Appendix F for Childhood Memories That Inspire]*

Do Your Best

We were glad to do our very best,
So, we kept pounding upon our chest.
When there are glad moments for us,
We take terms to help discuss.
Of course, there are grand moments in life,
When we are blessed with dodging struggle and strife.
I know this knowledge will help someone,
To do great service and say well done.

Exceedingly Good Effort

When your efforts are exceedingly good,
You can attract any neighborhood.
This is help for all fellow man,
It is great to help all people if you can.
We need to keep expressing this,
While holding our hands with a double fist.
These fine words we need to repeat,
Because it erases the words retreat.

August 24 – Curfew as a Youth

We were always accompanied by our big sister or older family members. We always had to get home before night as a youth. In my youth most events that were alright for youth attendance alone was a scheduled *[event]* in daytime.

August 25 – Follow the Leader Games

Follow the leader games here is described as a good stomping march with our cousins (Sophia and Jinnie Wade) and close neighbor's children. *[Also,]* big tin cans beaten with broom sticks made good music for following the leader.

August 26 – Telephone Use

There were very few telephones in our relative's possession in Longview, Texas. When I moved to Oklahoma City, my aunt

Sarah Bailey had a rotary phone. . . *[However,]* phone calls were not made very often. My friends, Mary Kate Dunn, Kansas Johnson, Myrtle Holloway, and all the students at Douglas High lived near our home in Oklahoma City. We attended the same church, so we saw each other often *[and did not need to make telephone calls]*.

August 27 – Accidental Home Fire

When I was about 15 years old, my grandmother Alice Edwards was making jelly on a wood fueled stove; hot cinders set ma and pa's house on fire. Pa was at his store about 1 ¼ miles away. Our house *[was]* about ¼ mile away on the next hill. We saw smoke and ran to help ma. [She was] still standing in her yard holding plum juice pan. She had fired shotgun in air to attract attention. Everyone near came to help. Well water was drawn; wet quilts were thrown on fire and some furniture. The ground was so hot that it was blue. Grandma was still standing in the fire scorched yard with her pretty grey hair scorched off on the back of her head. I ran to her and led her away to save her. The house completely burned.

August 28 – Box Socials and Pot Lucks

We once had box suppers at our elementary school in evening time. People would exchange food boxes and for financial purposes some boxes were sold. Everyone always watched certain good cook's boxes. . .use imagination here. Not too much programming *[took place]* here, just eating and socializing. Some story telling *[and]* a few dialogues, maybe.

Grandson's Wedding
(January 5th around 3:30pm)

I searched very hard for a lovely card
Yet, I found nothing on this great sod.
However, this is how I usually do things,
But I try hard with a powering.
So, it came to my mind, "In God We Trust,"
I could see very quickly a hundred dollars plus.
May you connect last with no end in years,
And we pray there will be no other tears.

There is Magic

Figure number three is magic,
Sad it cannot be set completely apart,
There has magic attraction coming from the heart.

When we think of three as just another number,
We can be sorely very wrong,
Speakers use it often because magic is very strong.

Surprising magic powers are numerous in three,
Like many other hidden truths on earth,
We always work to find viable rebirth.

So, work hard for this truth to be known,
This is a coined word of honor masked,
Good public speakers give it a full blast

August 29 – Angry with Dad (between 1927 & 1930)

We wanted to attend Heaven and Hell party at our school one evening. Coila T. and I were about 15 and 16 years old. Dad was not at home. Our stepmother Dora says you can go, but Mr. Bob is not going to like you to go. I am not going to tell you to go or stay at home. We went. *[In the interim]* papa shaved off his mustache. . .. And no sooner than *[when]* we arrived at the party, he walked up behind us and said "Are you girls ready to go back home?" Coila and I were so afraid. We were surprised that nothing happened.

August 30 – When Dad was Angry with Me

When I was 9 years old, I learned an Easter poem that I never recited. Before I was called on to recite my poem, I left church and ran home with "stage fright." Papa was embarrassed because I said, I am sick. Papa gave me Castor Oil to swallow. No, I did not like it.

August 31 – Outhouse Memory

Here is my chance to tell you that nobody we knew bought toilet tissue. Old Montgomery Ward and Sears catalogues were fun to see and read, wishing also during special sitting time in outhouse. We called these books guest or wish logs. If we were in need of secret comfort when walking through a forest. . . new soft leaves were plentiful; true. In those days there were not many people around *[in the forest]* to pester *[you]*. However, these *[soft leaves in the forest]* were not our habits; true.

Be Careful & Cards
(August 15, 2013)

Just be careful in all that you do.
The good things for life,
Will quickly ease you through.

Fair, you must always check.
What good thoughts in this life?
Will you make for a lucky "deck?"

A deck of fate has to do with cards.
While playing good games,
Many at gambling odds ran yards.

INDIAN SUMMER

September 1 – Labor Day Tradition
I remember families picnicking and celebrating by going fishing in Sabine River about three miles from our home; mostly White people. We sometimes went *[down to the]* May Hall Fruit gathering in *[the]* swamps, riding in our wagon. Our neighbors went also and traveled by wagon. May Hall trees grows in wet soggy swamps. The fruit is *[the]* size of cherries and very good. *[The fruit is]* yellow in color.

September 2 – VJ Day Memory
President Truman proclaimed September 2 as VJ Day. On September 2, 1945 aboard the battleship Missouri in Tokyo Bay, *[Japan]* allies and Japan signed surrender agreement. Richard and I had been married on year. We were at Utah's Bushnell General Hospital *[in Ogden City]* because Richard was injured on March 21, 1945 during World War II. He was in Germany. He was a sergeant during driving an M5 Tractor. His right ankle was fractured with machine vibration while bringing tractor to fast stop, eventually loosing [his] leg. While we were on an Ogden City Bus, a White man seeing Richard on crutches says "Now buddy,

what are you going to do?" Richard says "I am not going to do a dam thing. Your tax dollars are going to take care of me."

September 3 – My School Year Calendar

In Pleasant Elementary and in Greenville High school, all honored *[and]* important events *[were maintained on a calendar that was colorful]*. We made drawings and colored them for our bulletin board, *[added]* poems and written *[announcements]* were made for some events. This is the way we observed our school calendar.

September 4 – My First Day of School (1923 – 1924)

I was happy to let my teacher cousin Leala Bryant know how well I could read first week of school. . ... I was skipped from 1st grade to 3rd grade. I learned how helpful it was to read bill board signs while traveling. This anxiety made me an ardent speller at age seven.

September 5 – School Bully

Lorena Wright and Annie B. Harris *[were]* very much bullies. I can't remember which bully pushed sister Coila and started toward me to finish her bluffs. I let her have a taste of my lunch pail rim with one big swing. The decision to jump the Edwards girls was suddenly over for quite a while.

September 6 – School Recess
[There were several games and activities we would do at school recess]
1. Holding hands, making a large circle with one girl in center of ring. The girls would then move around singing ♪
    "Ring around Rosey pot full of poesies."
    Girl in center keeps eyes closed and tries to touch another girl to take her place.
2. Seventh grade basketball *[played by girls with]* uniforms of black cotton sateen bloomers made to look like skirts, worn with white middies blouses.
3. Two girls [with] hands held high together in archway form while about six or eight girls march through archway singing ♪
    "Hold up the gate, High as the sky,
    And let King George's horses by."
    Girls repeat *[this phrase and then what happens is left up to the imagination]*

September 7 – Our Playground Equipment
At Pleasant Green Elementary we had a basketball court. A croquet set, soft balls, and jump ropes. Our parents and teachers' association helped furnish playground equipment. Pleasant Green Elementary school was a few berry picking steps from our Pleasant Baptist Church.

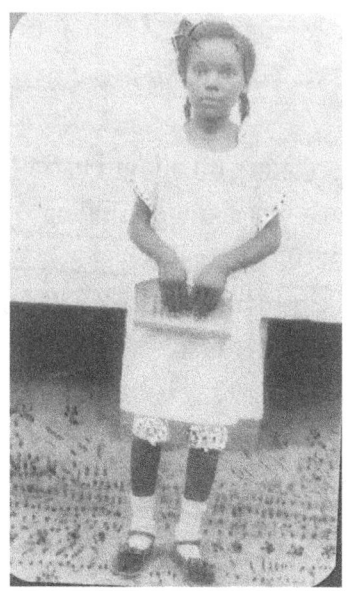
Myrtle 7 years old

September 8 – Our Parents Made Us Wear Stupid Things to School

Yes, old high-top shoes and long white union underwear that reached down into long black or brown stockings. Yes, Texas is a very cold state in winter. *[I must admit]* some stupid shoes were cute.

September 9 – The Smartest Kid in our School

Floree Jacobs of Greenville High, *[who lived in the]* Longview suburbs was very smart. Her mother, Edna Mae Jacobs, was my home economy teacher. Floree's parents worked diligently with her at all times. She was able to attend Bishop College in Marshall, Texas.

September 10 – The Dumbest Kid

Not a kid. We had an elderly gentleman in Pleasant Green Elementary school who had a learning disability. His name was Nathan Cotton. He always tried to say his name when asked. He would say Cot-cot-cot-un-ton. He was at least 65 years old.

September 11 – 7 Years Old

Sister Marie you know I do not like "French Pants." I am ashamed of these pants. *[This is the only childhood photo of Myrtle. She was seven years old]*.

September 12 – Teacher's Pet

Some distant cousins, Georgia and Will Dee Borders, always cried when they could not show good class work. Especially Georgia Mae, who was my full classmate and rival. They were still teacher's pets.

September 13 – Schools I Attended

1. Pleasant Green Elementary. *[Attended 1st through 7th grade – graduated]* 1930s
2. Greenville High School. *[Attended]* 8th thru 12th grades.
3. Douglas High School, Oklahoma City. Post High School; 12th grade. *[received a second HS Diploma]*
4. Langston University, Langston, Oklahoma 1938 – 1943.
5. Venice School of Business. Typing and shorthand, 1950.
6. UCLA Educational Sub

September 14 – Embarrassing School Moments

One of our school classmates was a distant cousin, very pretty long brown hair. We were rivals *[as]* students. Our teacher always had spelling matches with a lineup of kids *[in the]* 5th and 6th grades. After studying hard, it would be so embarrassing to miss a word of spelling correctly – so we worked harder and harder.

September 15 – The Grade School Teachers I Remember

1. Cousin Ambrose Taylor; tough teacher
2. Sam Vaughn, principal; started our girls basketball team
3. Mary Jane Bryant; our favorite elementary teacher
4. Leala Bryant; for a short time, elementary teacher.

September 16 – My Junior High & High School Teachers that I Remember

Green Ville High, near Longview, Texas
Edna Mae Jacobs, my sewing teacher. Some algebra.
Tourmae Sanders
Cousin Elzie Williams, geometry.

I must say that I could have appreciated a better foundation for math. I really feel cheated. Elzie was also physics *[teacher and]* in charge of school mechanics' shop.

Douglas High – Oklahoma City, Oklahoma
"Strict" Eugene Byrd – favorite
H.A. Berry

**Willie Myrtle Edwards
Post Graduate – 1936
Douglas High School**

Consuelo Tompkins (speech friend)
Margaret Dabney
G.S. Ricks
Henrietta Wright – Library
I.B. Burch

September 18 – My Typical School Day Outfit
Nice print or bright check gingham, long sleeves, long knit stockings. All leather high top shoes *[because]* Texas is a cold state. A bright knitted *[sweater]* a must. Heavy coats were always needed with big deep warming pockets for our hands. We had to wear long underwear in winter months. We had gloves if we could keep up with them.

September 19 – School Fights?
In some months of this book, I have written about hitting a school girl with my lunch pail. However, I never tried to be in a fight; for defense I remembered to surprise with an unexpected tough response.

Even male students at Douglas High *[in]* Oklahoma City accused me of having a defensive look. This was *[because]* I had not learned to trust people. My Texas social status was very different.

September 20 – My Worst Report Card
My grade school report cards – good always.

High school report card – good always.

Langston University – college was different. *[Report]* cards were not as good. I was competing with students who always had access to better classroom and all school facilities. I'm a college graduate and still feel "Blessed."

September 21 – I Had a Hero, Yes!

Sister Irene (Edwards) Walker, 1906 – 1991 was my hero; as early as I can remember she sent nice gifts to our family in Texas. After I moved to Oklahoma City to live with Aunt Sarah Bailey, she had me move to her home after I graduated from Douglas High *[in]* Oklahoma City. I stayed with my sister Irene until I married Richard Stewart *[on]* July 1, 1944.

September 22 – Hero Cont'd – Why Sister Irene E. Walker

It is gratifying to remember that my sister Irene really did what she could for me. Her spirit of giving was uplifting. This helped with courage to move on. Even after I married, she showed a special care for Richard and I. She always sent him shirts, jackets, neck ties or what she thought he would like for his birthday.

September 23 – The Best Teacher I Ever Had

Mrs. Consuelo Tompkins – My speech teacher at Douglas High School, Oklahoma City, was the best teacher that I have ever had. After I graduated from college (Langston University), she sent me to my first permanent teaching job in Choctaw, Oklahoma. She taught drama at Douglas High School also. As one of her good students I was able to win an award by orating James Weldon Johnson's "The Creation."

September 24 – What Made That Teacher Good?
Mrs. Consuelo Tompkins always did a follow-up on high school graduates. Her personality and teaching skills helped students to desire greater achievement in the graduate world and to move on up the ladder of success, while working in this universe for better living.

Mrs. Tompkins was also our next-door neighbor.

September 26 – My School Mascot?
I would like to trade the word mascot for motto; easy for me; say our high school motto. "Lifting As We Climb." I always wave at Douglas High saying, "I will always love you dear old high."

Our eighty-page Douglas High Annual was titled "The Mirror" submitted by my friend, Mattie B. White.

Lessons From Two Centenarians
(May 5, 2009)

One day two centenarians talked to me,
I tried to be interested as I could be.
They had stories from their lives inside,
They were thankful, and did not hide.
From early school days, to one hundred years,
They laughed while discussing early fears.
In our conversation my imagination grew,
Some fun things discussed; I would not do.
When I departed, I felt in my mind,
Those great centenarians were two of a kind.
With those conversations, I will remember,
Every lesson learned from January to December,
I smiled for a while, because I could see,
Every point discussed was educating me.

The Air Flight

The attendants worked so well,
We did not need adjustment cell.

I am a poet that let you know it,
And in each line, I aim to show it.

> Why worrying about this thousand-mile trip?
> People know it is cool to be hip.

September 27 – Sports I Played in School
Basketball, softball, croquet, high jumping and foot racing.

"Lunch Time Fun"
There was a shallow creek downhill from Greenville High School. We were caught by teacher Edna Mae Jacobs. While we were jumping the creek, one girl kept score of best jumper. Everyone involved was punished. There were about six of us girls. (smiles)

September 28 – My Favorite Sport to Watch (About 1931)
Basketball and softball. I remember how we loved to make our own softballs. With rapping strings, we also used a threaded needle to tack each string in place after wrapping the ball. Ball bats were plentiful, yes Papa Edwards' boards or good old forest sticks.

September 29 – A Relative – "I Misunderstood" (about 1979-1980)
I cannot stop thinking about our cousin Julia Hutchings-Earl, whose mother was my mother's relation (The Bryant family relatives of Texas Years ago). A dear cousin, Ira Bryant-Jones moved to Los Angeles, or just came on a visit to spend time with son John D. Jones. The traveling seemed too much for her. She called me; not feeling well. She passed suddenly. I called cousin Julia

Earl and thought she would inform me of the solemn ceremony. Julia gave me some jealous short talk with no sensible answer.

September 30 – Remembering a School Custodian (Texas)

No one especially, I only remember that each teacher took care of seeing that the school room was always maintained; students cleaned up our mess.

Later years, approximately 1943, when I was teaching at Dunjee High in Choctaw, Oklahoma, I do remember the custodian was good at some of the maintenance. But somethings made him untrustworthy. "True."

AUTUMN MONTH

October 1 – A Relative – Teacher Tricked by Students (Douglas High, about 1935-36)

One of my post graduate classes was English literature. Our teacher was Mr. H. A. Berry. There were two or three girls in class that carried on mischief. The ceiling above near a bathroom seemed to be very thin, we could hear flushing water above class room. Florida Geary and Nadine Baxter would say "Oh Mr. Berry *[you should]* be ashamed of yourself." He always had a sheepish grim so you could not tell what he thought. He could not handle them, so he ignored their crazy talk.

October 2 – The worst Thing a Teacher Did to a Student (Texas)

During my school days in Texas, teachers could whip students and most times, when told to parents by teachers, students got another whipping from parents. Worst thing this kind of action seemed to have *[was]* an uplifting morale effect on social behavior. Think about today's youth and adults. Standing on one foot in corner of class room was another bad punishment "we thought."

October 3 – School Lunches (Texas)

We had regular food that was available, rice, eggs, etc. Vegetables like baked potatoes or whatever was available on our farm, jelly and biscuits, fruit, etc. However, big hot breakfasts were made for us before we left for school. We always had early supper as we called it. The food that we had must have been very good for us. "We had all organic food."

October 4 – Crush on a Teacher?

No, I thought of Mr. Eugene Byrd as a very good teacher for post grad chemistry class. My first study in chemistry, Mr. Byrd was tall dark, about 170 pounds. He was domineering in perfect class work. Very quick to use the word "lip lazy," if you did not correctly pronounce words. He was very strict, dressed well, and wore only white shirts. Everyone liked and respected "Old Mr. Perfection."

October 5 – Special Leaf Raking and Burning?

Yes, there were beautiful trees around our home in Texas. And Papa cut Dog Wood bushes, tied them together into broom shapes for us to keep the yard of dirt (hard dirt) swept clean. When leaves got too plentiful, we swept them in piles and burned them. We had some bricks to outline our yard. Pretty gardenia bushes each side of our had dirt walk. These bushes of white blossoms had a very fragrant smell.

October 6 – Fun Playing in Leaves

Grandfather Clayborne Edwards' house on hill *[was]* about 4 blocks away by dirt road from our house. Hillside trees produced many leaves. Grandpa was Mason Lodge Treasurer in our community. We learned that he stored silver dollars between the wall planks. Our cousin Eldridge Price from Dallas, Texas was visiting Ma and Pa (his great-grand parents). Coila (12 years old) and Myrtle (10 years old) helps Eldridge stir the silver dollars in leaves on hill side, like robbers and get credit in finding this money. We always placed the money back between the wall boards. "We did not get caught."

October 7 – What Allowance Did We Get? ➔ None

Papa Edwards bought everything that we needed as children. But when we wanted extra change to spend as we chose, we knew a huckster, a man who sold vegetables and fruits in the streets. He charged community twenty cents on the dollar for what variety of fruits and vegetables that we bagged for his sales. When he passed through our community, we had our bags of produce ready. This man's name was Ed Mears.

October 8 – We had to Earn Allowance

Yes, we had to earn our extra change like October 7th story writes. Farming was an industry that had fixed job payment that varied in finance amounts. When crops were harvested, we were happy to choose our school clothes from whatever finance was available. However, we always had enough of everything.

October 9 – Teacher Dislike

I could never dislike any teacher. I may have dreaded going to Hobart Jarret's English class at Langston University. I may have regretted Edna Jacob's inability to teach Algebra; this is true.

Cousin Ambrose Taylor was tough in (7th grade) elementary school. I can appreciate him because he challenged me to work a problem that I did not like.

October 10 -- Why?

See October 9th date. It is hard on me this date in time to feel that some teachers did not understand me, because I think that they would have made better efforts in their instructions. Some teachers like Consuelo Tompkins, Ambrose Taylor, Louise Beasley, and a few others; would show interested students how to use most of their potentials.

The Antique Show (Revisited)[29]

The antique show is really something to see

For people who love the antique show
Many associate old-time gifts to people they know.

Gifts maybe from mother, dad, sister or brother
But their gifts on display were like no other.

Gadgets of all sort, judged by anxious inspectors
Making values on old gadgets with disgruntle rejector.

We view many gadgets with poor valued taste,
Working careful with old relics before they go in waste.

---

29 This is the second of two poems that Myrtle Stewart wrote with the same title. The Antique Show appears earlier in this publication.

> I love to visit the antique show,
> With values galore that we should know.

October 11 -- Story about a Mouse in the House
We always caught mice when we found them in our house. Mice always got beaten up with a broom. Mice and small snakes in our yard and near our house did not have a chance; not too often. But think how much fun this was for children hungry for good fun and games.

October 12 – A change of Pace Began – 1935
Memory about a Bat in the House.
I slightly remember a bat getting into our house. I was very frightened because they carry small insects and disease (see October 13, 1935).

After I became 17, I moved to Oklahoma City and life was very different with Aunt Sarah (Craig) Bailey. She was very strict. After post-graduation from Douglas High, I moved with my sister Irene E. Walker. She helped me get a job to prepare for Langston College.

October 13 – Strange Animals in the House
We experienced snakes, rats, and mice in our territory. Our papa safely spread rat and mouse glue in outside entrances. Of course, every now and then small intruders made their way in. Our step mom helped us broom whip a strange bat in our house. This we had never seen before.

October 14 – How We Got to and from School
Pleasant Green Community Elementary school building was [*approached*] only through a few berry hopping trails. And through a small safe piney forest, then suddenly (across a well graded "dusty" county road) this neatly built school was our destination.

For high school we had to walk three miles to our sister community of Greenville High, [*come*] rain or shine. Papa Edwards bought a new 26 Ford in later years [*and*] he took us to school in bad weather.

October 15 – A Good School –No Tease
No, I was very well adjusted here because I was never ready for a big tease. Our school students were much nicer to each other during my school days and certainly much more protective to each other.

October 16 – About Losing a Baby Tooth
I always tried to pull my own teeth because papa scared me when I was small. I did not want his hands in my mouth any more. He would see me afterwards saying, "open your mouth Myrt. Now, when did you lose that tooth?"

October 17 – Loss of Something Important
I was a member of a drama club in Oklahoma City at Douglas High. [*I was also in the*] Douglas High speech club. I won a Women's Christian Temperance Union (WCTU) Black and Gold pin in an oratorical contest. My darling teacher [*for the*

club] was Mrs. Consuelo Tompkins. I lost the WCTU pin. This pin became more valuable to me in mind when I found WCTU listed in World Book Encyclopedia, History of women's clubs. According to their objectives, *[the WCTU was influential in combating the impact of alcohol on families and society, support for the 18th Amendment, labor law and prison reform, and suffrage].*

October 18 – U Broke Something That Belonged to Someone Else

Yes! When our family was visiting cousin Lattie Bradford, one of our mother Lucy's favorite cousins, my father said that I broke a bushel basket of eggs. I was about 4 or 5 years old. Evidently these cousins did not let papa whip me. I do not remember that "egg basket breaking."

October 19 – Where Did My Clothes Come from?

Papa Rober (Bob) Edwards bought very good non-fading fabrics for sister Marie Edwards to make our clothes. Our shoes were of the very best quality also. Papa did not believe in old hand-me-down clothes. He always looked for "guarantee label."

There was a search for written guarantees on everything that our papa purchased. Perkins Brothers, Hopkins and Stuckey's Haliburtons, Ray Rembert's were our stores for good clothes.

October 20 – A favorite Fall Memory

The leaves were fading and falling. The wind was high and wild, twirling; red, gold, and amber leaves rolling. Exciting to any country child. Yes, these were beautiful and exciting times for me. Looking through the forest to find pretty colored and fading leaves to pin on my straw field hat was fun. I enjoyed pulling off my shoes to wade in the cool water running over the multi-colored rocks. When I went home, I enjoyed writing verse about the babbling brook.

> The leaves were fading and falling.
> The wind is rough and wild.
> If you do not like the weather,
> Put on more clothes my child.

October 21 – Picking Apples

We had one large apple tree of mellow tasting greenish white apples. Very few on tree. We had fig trees all over edge of back yard. My grandfather Clayborne Edwards had a peach orchard. People came from miles around to pick peaches and share.
We enjoyed picking black berries under edge of peach orchard. Wild plum trees and berry patches were plentiful everywhere in our community. We never had to buy fruit.

October 22 – The Farthest I ever Ran or Walked.

We the Edwards youth walked about one quarter miles to Pleasant Green Elementary school. When we finished elementary grades (1st grade through 7th grade), we walked three miles to Greenville High school. White students passed us riding in their school bus.

After I graduated, I moved to Oklahoma City to become a post graduate in Douglas High. After graduating again, I enrolled in Langston University for four years (1938 – 1942).

October 23 – Douglas High School Had Cheerleaders

Yes, Douglas's cheerleaders wore grey sweaters with red strip trim pleated skirts that were gray.

>Douglas, Douglas, Rah! Rah! Rah!
>Do your stuff, right where you are!

October 24 – School Cheers

Dad Edwards took us to Marshall, Texas when sister Marie was a freshman at Wiley College to see Wiley College and Bishop College play football. I do not think I was more than 8 years old. I remember some of the yells and cheers the pep squad enjoyed doing.

>Bishop College yells… "Sting ♪ them ♪ hornets."
>Wiley College yells and cheers … "Yea… Big team, big team – Wiley Wild Cats, fight, fight, fight."
>[Also,] we had a cousin in Marshall, Texas. Her name was cousin Donie. She gave us our first taste of jello.

October 25 – Homecoming

Greenville High school always invited Longview High school for football and scholastic rivalry in math, spelling, and handcraft exhibits. Parents were judges [who] issued blue, yellow, and white ribbons for prizes.

Greenville High has been renamed N.E. Williams High school in honor of our in-law uncle Ned Williams. His wife was my mother Lucy's Aunt Ada Williams.

October 26 – Pleasant Green Baptist: First Sunday in August Special Homecoming

We always celebrated the first Sunday in August as homecoming. This was a time when everyone far and near come back home to our "Annual Revival." Everyone seemed to buy and dress their best. Food was brought to church grounds in trucks and huge boxes. Everyone wanted friends and relatives to taste their food after church services. Many people on church grounds did not see inside church. There were many people who treated this occasion like a picnic. This revival lasted one week. The last time I attended this occasion my daughter [*Marquetta*] was about 4 years old.

October 27 – High School Extra Curricular Activities

Nonother than special holiday programs, speeches, and short plays in drama class; public speaking; sewing club. I helped in organization of "joke" sheet for our annual "The Mirror" at Douglas High, Oklahoma City.

October 28 – Costume Dressing

During a spring festival, maybe Easter time, some family members made me a costume rose dress [*with*] white, pink, and green crepe paper. My skirt was pink crepe paper. My arms were covered with green leaves. "The Rose."

"Rose" Costume

October 29 – A Memory of Being Very Scared (about 1927-1928)

Colia and Myrtle were scared when papa left us in our car parked outside of his favorite store, "Ray Remberts." A little white girl on side walk saw us in car and she may have tried to talk to us. However, we greeted her with wide twisted up lips. When she ran and told a white man who looked like a grand-father, Coila and Myrtle laid down between car seats. She made noise from side walk saying, "Hey girls! Hey girls!" But girls did not answer. We were very glad when she and the old man left. "We did not tell papa."

October 30 – Halloween Fun

There were a plenty of pumpkins around in fields, so it was easy to make lanterns. However, we played tricks on each other for fun. Most of our activities during holidays we practiced at school. We had short plays and games during assembly time in school. Many times, best pictures for the occasion or for the time was drawn and presented to the teacher. These decorations stayed on display until new holidays demanded a change of picture in class room.

October 31 – A True Story – A Special Halloween Memory"[30]

On Halloween night in the 30's, papa told us girls that he had a large bent root near roadside in from of our house. He threw a large black coat over it to make it look like a man. Papa left

---

30 This story is similar to one recorded by Myrtle Edwards on April 1.

the house with his gun. Within two hours we heard a gunshot. We all ran out of the house with our step-mom Dora. We could barely see the black coat object turned over. Mrs. Dora screamed "Oh somebody done shot Mr. Bob." Shortly after prank, Mr. Bob came stepping with "Big Laugh."

HUNTING SEASON

November 1 – Did We Tell Ghost Stories?
My brother Rogers told a Gabriel story; a preacher called Gabriel to blow his horn. Two boys climbed in a tree near church and blew their horn. . .. during a dark rainy night [*while church service was being held*]. Preaching for Gabriel became intense, boys became intense for tooting horns. Suddenly all congregation of people ran out of church. . . preacher finds himself alone…he ran for the church door but was caught by his big black scissor tail coat and by a big nail. The preacher started screaming – "Please turn me loose Gabriel!" He ran out of church door into dark rainy night, he fell into a well. "Ole-lush-a-loom" as he bobbed up and down in the well, he said loudly, "Into hell as I expected."

November 2 – A Ghost Story
Only a deep forest story about a man running from what he felt was a ghost. When he got tired, he sat down on a stump; suddenly the ghost touched him on his shoulder saying "there is no one here except us." This happened about three times in "the stump rest act for the man." The man's fourth move was to jump

in the lake. The ghost was waiting at the lake bank. . . The ghost says, "There is no win, _____ [???]."[31]

November 3 – Strangest Thing We Saw in the Sky

True. When I was about 11 years old, there must have been a circus coming to town; giant flood lights were circled throughout the clouds, while friends and relatives were traveling in wagons from town. These huge flood lights could be seen for many miles by people who had no idea the reason. So, everyone started confessing, thinking that judgement day was at hand. People were crying, saying to each other "I told you that I have been good. Some people acclaimed to have seen an angel feather. Big flood lights had a frightening effect on people's minds because the lack of communication was present in all rural.

November 4 – Keeping Our House Warm as a Child

We had wood burning stoves. Our nearby forest had a wealth of good wood; oak, pine, sweet gum, and plum trees. Wood was cut by family members who could use a saw and axe. Pine trees has [sic] a sap that will burn like gasoline, so getting houses warm was no problem. Sweet gum (when hacked) would produce a yellowish clear gum that when picked from trunk of sweet gum tree, could be chewed as gum. It was good also.

---

31 The editors could not determine what the final words were on this entry.

November 5 – The President in Office When I was Born

Woodrow Wilson was president [*from*] 1917 – 1921. On April 6, 1917 Congress passed a joint resolution declaring war on Germany. On February 26, 1917, Willie Myrtle Edwards was born. In February 1917 Germany sank five American ships (unarmed passenger ships). This helped to anger Americans. But on June 1914 a single act, the shooting of Archduke Francis Ferdinand, heir to the throne of Austria-Hungary (and his wife), both were killed. This marked the outbreak of World War I. A Serbian student or [*one*] who lived there killed Ferdinand. Austria-Hungary declared was on Serbia to begin World War I. Other countries, [*to include*] France, USA, and England joined the fight for international reasons.

November 8 – A Purchase that I Regret

Yes, more than once. A quick use of telephone once saved me from one sale that I felt that I did not need… A set of books. I still try to find use for regretted purchases around my house. Some of these – yes, some of these gifts became gifts for someone in need of them.

November 9 – When on Car Trips, Did I play "Car Games?"

When on car trips, we did more singing, and sleeping at early ages. Counting cars we pass, etc. But I always thought that I needed to be crafty and dabble with needle and thread or something related. When we traveled by wagon, counting shooting stars across the sky was our best fun because we always made a wish immediately. The wish was always about true boy-friend, with a successful marriage.

November 10 – My First Watch

I purchased my first watch when I was teaching at Shoemack High school in Colbert, Oklahoma. I bought a Bulova watch from Zales Jeweler's in Oklahoma City, Oklahoma. I wore this watch many years.

November 11 – An Armistice Day Memory: World War I

When I was 5 or 6 years old, my papa Bob Edwards would take us to City of Longview to visit mother's sister Sarah (Craig) Bailey. I can remember peeping at our deceased Uncle Leander Evans (Aunt Sarah's first husband) steel hat and army uniform. (See *May 16 -- Military Experience of Someone in Our Family, and September 2 -- VJ Day*).

In World War II when battle ceased between US and Japan, Richard and I had been married about 16 months. Richard was on crutches when we were in Ogden City, Utah. Everyone was happy and friendly about the end of war. Trains were tooting and bells were ringing all day long. City bus rides were free for us.

November 12 – My Prized Possession as a Child

My chocolate doll, and many pieces of material to cut and sew. I needed to possess materials and equipment for crafts, all kinds for drawing, also for drawing and coloring. There was not much else from which to choose.

November 13 – Standing Up in My Beliefs

I wanted to use sewing machine but others thought [a] 12-year-old did not need to use sewing machine. Never-the-less, I managed to make patterns, hide them, and sew anyway. Coila, my sister, only 1½ or 2 years older than I, was my pest in trying to tattle about my sewing. Since we have been adults, I have sewn for her. I proved that I was old enough to sew.

November 14 – Feeling a Hatred for Someone

No, not really. I dreaded their presence because of their mean and bully attitude. However, I always managed to stay away from "bully people." I also had to extend a few "back off" surprises!

November 15 – The Best Birthday Present

I have received many nice birthday presents. My sister Irene gave me a red jewelry box (exclusive kind). A friend gave an Amethyst birth stone ring in 1940!

November 16 – Injustice Done

Yes, I was traveling on Oklahoma and Kansas Trailway Bus; I was one of the earliest passengers for seating. Every time a white person boarded the bus my seat was changed. I was a student at Langston University. This action did not last long because this bus company, Oklahoma and Kansas Trailways and Traveling

Tours" were changed.[32] All bus fares were refunded to people who had to give up seats for others.

November 17 – Poison Ivy and Poison Weed

Poison Ivy vine grows in Texas and Oklahoma (and also other southern states). We enjoyed looking for nettle bushes with edible nut goodies to enjoy if you cared to fight with bush and hull stickers. Sometimes poison Ivy was touched, which gave a reddish rash on skin. Then, it had to be treated with a special skin lotion to stop rash and itch.

November 18 – Memorable Birthday Cake

I cannot remember a birthday cake. However, my sisters, Marie and Alice (oldest sisters) were very good young lady cooks; and they made some surprises for us. I can still see the special white cake (they once made) with pretty green rose leaf decoration over the white cake with icing that I use to tip by and touch to taste. They would say "Myrt did it."

November 19 – Recurring Dreams

It seems that I always dreamed of our main house entrance door

---

32 Jim Crow laws were state and local laws that mandated racial segregation in public facilities and transportation, which started as early as the 1870s, was eventually extended to include interstate trains and buses. These harmful laws were certainly in effect during the time of Myrtle Edwards' Trailways bus ride, which must have occurred in the late 1930s. However, it is unclear how bus fares were refunded to people who had to give up seats for others since Jim Crow laws were enforced until 1965.

falling and to secure it I had to push it. I always dreamed of falling in Ma Edwards' water well that was at the edge of her side porch. I always dreamed of riding on train. I guess because I could hear it a few miles away.

November 20 – Youth Hair Styles – Longview, Texas

As early as I can remember, my sister Alice or Marie platted my hair in one long plat tied with ribbon on end. Sometimes my hair was platted in two or three plats with ribbon ties. Three plats were a specialty. Very few times hanging curls were made.

November 21 – Talk About Influential People over My Life

More than one person had a big influence over my life. My sister, Robbie Irene Edwards-Walker was number one in my life. As early as I can remember she worked and shared her earnings with our family *[and]* with pretty hats especially. Also, many other gifts (i.e., books). My sister helped me get jobs in Oklahoma City, helped me to start a savings at downtown Oklahoma City Post Office 1935-1938.[33]

---

33 The **United States Postal Savings System** was a postal savings system signed into law by President William Howard Taft and operated by the United States Post Office Department, predecessor of the United States Postal Service, from January 1, 1911 until July 1, 1967 (References: Postal Savings System by United States Postal Service, July 2008 and Postal Savings System Act of June 25, 1910, P.L. 61-268; 36 Stat. 814).

November 22 – What I Was Doing When John F. Kennedy was Assassinated

I was listening to radio news report while keeping up with a few house chores. This was time for tele-viewing just hoping that the news was not true about assassination of our 35th president.

November 23 – Weather Related School Cancellation

A few times, I remember heavy rains swelled our large creek about 2½ blocks down our big grassy hill. These were times when very little going in this direction were made. The water run off was very swift and we would go downhill to watch the fast-moving currents. There were other roads to help us escape this hazard.

November 24 – Thanksgiving Tradition

Many times, we visited Mother Lucy's Cousin Sicily and David Jones. Over and through the woods by our grandparents' house we ran; cousin David and cousin Sicily had open arms for everyone. No special invitation was given. This well-kept bungalow was always full of the best of guest [sic]. I like to think of the times that papa would say "Cousin Sicily is coming by to borrow Lucy's hat that is in the hallway truck." When I learned about mother Lucy's hat, it became my pleasure to take a good look [at] this pretty fine straw hat, "light brown in color [with] pretty small flowers."

November 25 – Our Thanksgiving Foods

Most Thanksgiving days we had baked hen with cornbread dressing. Corn was home grown [*but*] (rice had to be bought). Baked goose, rooster or turkey that Ma Edwards raised. Many kinds of vegetables, potato pies, pumpkin pies or pudding. Baked cushaw (a large striped gourd like fruit) seasoned with brown sugar and spice.

November 26 – A Thanksgiving Memory

It was fun for me to draw objects and figures depicting holidays and special occasions. Turkey goose and rooster drawing first figures. Our parents loved to cook big white goose for some occasions. To make the goose fat, papa would put goose in cage. It was fun to watch him <u>nail</u> the <u>goose</u> webbed feet to floor or cage to keep goose from eating his own waste. We had large fruit orchards. I can remember one cousin visiting us [*who*] ate ½ bushel of apples. I do not wish to write his name. We girls fed him apples for fun.

November 27 – Ice Skating Memories

We did very little outside activities during icy days in Texas. We were always looking out to see it snow. [*There were*] not too many heavy snow days in South-East Texas. We had some very cold winters when the heavy rains came; sometimes icicles would line the tree limbs. Icicles tasted good picked off limbs and twigs when papa was not looking.

Papa always made snow ice cream for us. Sometimes we had fun leaping off our big "L" porch and falling in big piles of snow – "This was a sneak."

November 28 – Hobbies or Collections as a Youth (1920s & 30s in Oklahoma and Texas)

Making doll clothes and doll houses, picking wild flowers and attaching them to my hat. I once enjoyed making and collecting pretty handkerchiefs. But thanks God for facial tissue. We had fun cutting out paper dolls and mounting them on cardboard. I always enjoyed making crepe paper roses. I learned to make hooked rugs in Douglas High [in] Oklahoma. I made my sister Irene a hooked rug once in later years.

November 29 – Our Parents Ailment Remedies for US (Medications)

Yes, Castor Oil, Black Draught Turpentine on Sugar (for colds, etc.). Kerosine Oil for insect bites. Camphor Oil for rubbing skin after bites of insect. Soda for stomach ache. And a good whipping if acting bad!

November 30 – Famous People and Places

I looked at two people of special recognition.

1. Jessie Brewer Park [in] Los Angeles. Displays life's story and photo of Mr. Brewer. This was the game sight for "86 World Olympics" and other big games.

My mother's cousin Jessie Brewer, Los Angeles Police Chief. I met him at his sister's funeral, made myself acquainted. He says, "Yes, Willis Craig was my grand-father. I said, "No, Willis Craig was my grand-father." He says "is that the way it was?" I said "Yes, three brothers, Willis, Noah, and Louis Craig. I went to school with Noah Craig's grandchildren.

2. Uncle Ned Williams of N. E. Williams High school in Longview, Texas suburb. [He was] widely known and recognized as an educator.

WINTER – THE CHRISTMAS SEASON

December 1 – Bad Experience with a Hair Cut?
Yes, when I was about 11 years old, my sister Marie cut my hair off for a good barb; she had me wearing a cap every day to keep papa from it. My hair grew back before he noticed it.

December 2 – My Favorite Movie Star
Lena Horne (actress). She has been an activist, strong in her belief for civil rights. I had two magazines with star's photographs, and hers was the one I gazed on and adored.

December 3 – Why?
Lena Horne was a civil rights fighter. She always petitioned for better service in hotels and restaurants for minorities.

December 4 – When I Was in a Life-Threatening Situation
I believe that I have been in some life-threatening situations, through witnessing come ailments, which I have watched and

cared for earlier. I was in hospital in the 1960's for an operation that may have saved me to this last 20 years. I am thankful now at 79 years. By the time this book changes hands, I have faith that I will be 80 years old. "Thank God!" I am reading this again (today I am 81 years, June 1st, 1998).

"October 1978, Ah! Ah!"

December 5 – Yes, I Have Some Younger Pictures

Not many, if any childhood pictures were taken.[34] I have some pictures in front, middle, and back of this book from later years.

December 6 – How My Name Was Chosen

Some in family said I was named Willie after the evangelist Rev. Willie Nixon. My sister Alice said that I was named Myrtle after a distant relative named Myrtle O'Neal. I do remember playing with her children; one young girl was named Olivia O'Neal.

---

34 Only one as a child at the beginning portion of this book. Several as a young adult and many as a senior.

These O'Neal's lived across the street from Aunt Sarah (Craig) Bailey in Longview, Texas. Papa always left us (Coila and I) in Aunt Sarah's care while he shopped for groceries.

December 7 – A Pearl Harbor Day Memory (June 1, 2000)

Yes, retired Mailing Requirements Clerk Arthur J. Copper was recently awarded the prestigious Pearl Harbor Survivors License plate, given to the remaining veterans of December 7, 1941 attack. Arthur Copper was aboard USS Tennessee on the day Pearl Harbor was attacked by the Japanese, serving as OC third class[35] in ammunition bay *[of the ship]*. He escaped unharmed. The honorary license plate was presented to Copper by the State of California. He is one of less than 600 remaining survivors to receive this auto license plate.

December 8, 1925 -- Our Favorite Store to Browse in as a Child

Father Robert Edwards traveled to Longview, Texas as often as his family of four girls needed to shop for the home and for each

---

35 OC third class (also known as OC 3rd class), is called Officer Cook 3rd Class Petty Officer. The Messman/Steward Branch of the Navy was the most segregated part of the United States Navy. It was composed mostly of African-Americans and Filipinos whose primary responsibility was to serve officers in all housekeeping type duties. As it turns out, in World War II (WW II), the Navy had too many African-Americans in this branch. As such, the Navy also deployed them in other activities such as combat functions.

other. [*Oh, by the way*] Sister Irene ran away at age 18 to live in Longview with Aunt Sarah (Craig) Evans. The stores that we were privileged to visit and browse were Ray Remberts Grocery Store, McEinis and Haliburtons, Rawley Drug Store, Hopkins and Stuckey's. We lived about eight miles from Longview.

Wagon traveling seemed very slow, but even traveling was entertainment for children who were lucky enough to go anywhere from the "Piney Woods" . . . We were happy![36]

December 9 – What Did We Like to Look at There?

Shoes, hats, clothing, etc. Toys of course. Our father always bought the best of clothing with fast color guarantee; real leather shoes. We really liked to look at hats.

December 10 – Something I Designed, Built or Made as a Youth

I designed pretty doll dresses, [*and*] card board furniture for doll house for every room. Card board Christmas trees were made as well as Christmas decoration. Sun bonnets were very popular. I always tried to make a bonnet. We had fun designing our straw sun hats with white daisies and wild hill side fern.

---

36 The wagon was probably a Buckboard Wagon, which is generally drawn by one or two horses or similar farm animals. Average speed of a horse drawn wagon would be 5 to 8 MPH depending on the load, weather, and road conditions. Accordingly, it would take Papa Edwards and four girls approximately one hour to travel from home to Longview, Texas.

December 11
We once had a flower garden pageant at school. All clothes were made in flower pedals and leaves from Dennison Crepe paper.[37]

December 12 – We Did Not Put Up an Early Christmas Tree
Pa Edwards watched his pretty pine trees and cedars near our home. The most beautiful majestic Holly tree at the edge of my father's property and his first cousin Walter Wade's property still rest in my mind. This beautiful tree stood more than one story high. We struggled every "Yuletide" while hacking on these pretty branches to decorate our house with branches and red berries.

December 13 – Christmas Decoration (1920 – 1934)
We cut holly sprigs from our cousin Walter Wade's majestic holly tree for our house décor. There were several kinds of cedar and fir trees in our forest. We used Pine tree decorations. We did not do much of this kind, but we made colorful paper bells and paper rings out of any kind of paper.

December 14 – Christmas Tree Decor
We cut fresh holly tree or the twigs for tree decoration. We learned how to make crepe paper chains to decorate our tree and windows. Construction paper was used for figures that we liked to be on tree.

---

37 The Dennison Manufacturing Company made crepe paper and tissue paper, which was used in the early 20th century for home décor, Christmas ornaments, and children's stage costumes in place of fabric.

December 15

We did not hang Christmas stockings. We used shoe boxes. These boxes were filled with fruit and candy; better than today's fruits. We always expected a doll. We could smell the fruit many days before Christmas. So, we figured who "Santa" was. Cake baking gave our home a festive atmosphere. We were happy.

December 16

Our grandmother Alice (Wade) Edwards made Tea cakes, jellies, and jams. Life styles were different. I remember a beautiful pink slip she let me wear when I was 15.

[*Grandfather*] Pa Edwards [*was a*] "very jolly" man [*and*] everyone loved [*to call him*] Uncle Clayborne. He had a grocery store. I thought he had the best red salmon, coconut candy, and old fashion peanut patties candy.

I still see in my mind, the white [house] on the hill with Ma and Pa, with a big swing on porch, pretty yard of all kinds of flowers. Bridal wreath bushes with long stems of tiny white flowers. I use to tie these wreaths around my head. [*I can still see the*] rose bushes and honeysuckle vines.

December 17 – The Neatest Thing I Remember Giving to my Mom

Mother Lucy (Craig) Edwards went home triumphant when I was 2 years old. So, the time must have been about 1919. Story on January 1st of this book (please see).

I can remember (very slightly) the beloved teacher Mary Jane Bryant bringing flowers in her buggy to our house [*after my mother went home triumphantly*]. This is a faint memory that family members spoke about when I was very young. "Myrtle, do you remember Cousin Mary Jane Bryant? Distant cousin; everyone [*is*] related."

December 18 – The Neatest Present I Gave My Dad

I remember sending father money after I started working during the 1940's while teaching at Dunjee High school in Choctaw, Oklahoma, about 16 miles from Oklahoma City. I learned to drive Richard Stewart's '41 Chevrolet, to drive 32 miles round trip daily. I tried to be as nice to my family as they were to me. Since I spent most of Langston University years with sister Irene, I bought her a rain coat. She [*also*] purchased a lovely red wool robe on my Rothchild's store account.

December 19 – My Best Christmas Present

The best presents that I ever had or received was Wilton R. Stewart and Marquetta (Stewart) Brown; my lovely son and daughter. Wilton was lot of fun and joy. Marquetta was very cuddly and sweet.

[*As little girls*] we received pretty dolls, like other little girls. Dolls were special to us. We had black dolls that I wish I could find for keeps. Dad's house burned about 1949.

Baby Marquetta could wiggle her head down between elbows and side as if she was hiding. She was so cute.

December 20 – The Worst Christmas Present

Santa brought Coila Terry and I some black dolls. We did not appreciate those dolls enough at that time. We were ages 8 and 10 years. I feel that those dolls would be collectors' items today. Sister Coila may have one or both of those dolls today. My father's house burned years ago, about 1949. . . In my mind I think of some valuable keepsakes may have been destroyed. The Blue Book Speller is an important antique today and also the First Grade Primer.

December 21 – Santa Claus Experience

Sister Coila T. and Myrtle could find some of Santa's Christmas gifts by the good smelling fruits, candy, and nuts that were floating in country air. These kinds of products had not been seen in a year. . . We spent Christmas Eve night at grand ma and pa's house. We tried to be nice as we realized ma Edwards needed to retire in bed early. . . We went to bed early also. So, she placed her gifts under the pretty tree from grand pa's forest [*that was*] loaded with pine and cedar trees. We could hear ma moving around slowly. . . "We shook with tickles."

December 22 – Talk About a Special Service

Our church had a yuletide program. I recall a little boy stepping upon stage; his speech titled "Santa Claus is here." But when Santa came from behind the Christmas tree on stage the little boy ran off stage; his mom could not get him to respond. We all were young but we had to speak on stage. Although, we laughed [at the little boy,] our lips were trembling and we had shaking legs as we spoke on stage. [*We*] felt guilty. Somewhere in this book, I embarrassed my papa by running back home to keep from speaking my speech.

December 23 – When We Were To Open Our Presents.

Christmas morning. . ... the beds became really tumbled because we were awake early of course. . . but dared not hop up too soon. It was noted that we did not like early rising. "We did the tip around" first to check and see if anyone else was up; sometimes hopping back in bed of course until that long-awaited hour for us to be glad and joyful. "True"

Yes, presents were opened quickly.

December 24

December 25 – Remembering A Best Christmas

As a child all were good. We could even smell Christmas before the date. We learned later the fruit and candy sweet smell was coming from garage and from house attic where papa had stashed it. Even the taste of fruit is different now. We received new clothes that were not in Christmas boxes.

Special cake making took place, everything was good. We knew of no other kind of celebration and all children were in church participating in programs on Christmas day.

December 26 – other Christmas Memories
Hello Ruby, "Christmas Give." So (Myrt), since I said it first you should have a gift in your pocket for me. Sometimes this brought friendly arguments if not a laugh for jokes in saying who said Christmas give first.

This became a real game for "yuletide fun."
  "Hello, Christmas give – I said it first, now where is my gift?"

December 27 – Wedding Anniversary
I do not remember attending any wedding anniversaries. We attended many beautiful weddings when I was a child. It seems that some of our relatives were always getting married. Games were played, celebration came soon after on that same day or night. Games that were played included:

1. Musical chairs. Nine or ten chairs were placed in middle of largest room. Eleven people had to play marching around chairs to music [*and*] as soon as music stopped, quickly people would sit down. The one person who did not grab a chair [*to sit*] was a looser and out of the game.
2. Gossip game. First person tells short story to available person who passes the gossip to one other person. . . You see, the words are never the same with the last gossiper.

December 28 – Origin of Family Name
Research; Webster II College Dictionary. Thus, Edward means rich guardian. The "ead" equals the word rich and the "ward" equals the

word guard. This comes from the Anglo-Saxons, who settled in Britain from Germany in the 5th and 6th Century.

The Chinese people were the first known to acquire more than one name. The family name placed first – Edwards, was the name of eight different Kings who ruled England in the 12th century to the 17th century.

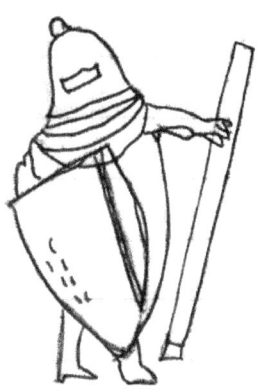

Our grandfather, Clayborne Edwards, whose original home was West Virginia, was a slave and may have taken his family name from that of the slave owner. Undoubtedly, the slave owner's ancestry was English.

December 29 – Something Else About My Childhood

Yes, I grew up, very quiet speaking, with no one to direct me in a special desired direction; however, well cared for. I always wanted to be famous, and outstanding. I always tried to write poems. I loved poems about the Babbling Brook and Multi-Colored fall trees! While surrounded by natural beauty, satisfied my feeling for beauty and joy, with a quite country atmosphere, I was able to work and think positively about what I wanted to do in life. I felt that I was hampered for a good chance, but I am "Thankful Anyway" at this point and time – 84 years old is a blessing for me.

December 30 – New Years' Resolution

Sometimes I made New Year's resolutions; however, seldom as a youth. I still make a list of things I need to do for annual success. Library visits, poems, collecting and especially uplifting quotations and proverbial [*thoughts*]– "I like."

"Mediation is Consolation" (my quote). As a youth I always thought about the kind of seamstress I would like to be. Also, one of my dreams was to be excellent at everything. "All of the tasks above for me even now, – waters down depression for me.

Please remember also that the power and strength to meditate is a blessed gift for survival.

December 31 – Special New Year's Memories

We liked this quote.
> "On New Year's Eve a band of brothers, the bear, the wolf, the fox, and others all met in peace in the Big Black Forest."

This quote came from a story book that our sister Irene sent to us when we were children.
> "Like many other people today, we believe that Black Eyed Peas and Hog Jowls was to be cooked for annual good luck!"

Everyone in our community had made their hog killing parties a success, by asking each neighbor for help in killing hogs, hanging to drain while cleaning and trimming afterwards. Scraping all hair off hide. Each person took a little piece of hog home, snoot, tail, or something – "True."

EPILOGUE

**"I'm sitting here writing (Sgt.), all about you,
Dear Sergeant, this poem is very true."**

Our mother's survival of World War II is a testimony to the power of faith, love, and optimism. Our father, Richard Stewart, for whom the poem A Gentle Giant was written, was a Purple Heart decorated World War II veteran.

During World War II, Richard participated in the Rhineland Campaign in the European Theatre of Operations (ETO) from November 1944 to March 1945. He was assigned to the 686th Field Artillery Battalion (Negro) as a section chief charged with supervising a Howitzer squad in combat. His unit was added to the Army's artillery strength for the final attack against Germany. Because of his combat service, Sergeant (Sgt.) Stewart received a battlefield commission as a 2nd Lieutenant in the US Army. However, due to the racial climate in the United States, his commission was later revoked after being hospitalized.

Injustices enacted against African-American soldiers in WWII are "not part of the public narrative, and generally are reserved for personal reflection as is found in autobiographies and memoirs" (Hunter & Rollins, 2015, p. 273). The practice of segregating black people in the United States extended into the military medical system (Marble, 2012). This segregated treatment for Blacks was usually substandard. In support of segregation, "there were separate blood banks, hospitals or wards, medical staff, barracks and recreational facilities for Black soldiers" (Clark, 2020, Para 4).

On the morning of March 25, 1945, at 0600 hours, in Rhine Valley, under the cover of darkness, Richard was driving down the highway at 80 miles per hour as part of a convoy of M-4 High-Speed Tractors. While trying to stop the tractor he was driving from hitting refugees located on both sides of the road, he fractured both of his ankles.

As a result of unit 4189 Army Hospital Plant discrimination practices requiring White soldiers to be triaged before Black soldiers, Sgt. Stewart did not receive medical treatment in a timely manner. His right leg was initially amputated to just below his knee; however, bacterial infection permitted gangrene to set in. Ultimately, a second amputation to just below his hipbone had to be done to save his life. WWII medical statistics document that the survival rate for lower extremity amputation was 4.7%, and the overall survival amputation rate was 2.5% (Rostker, 2013).

EPILOGUE

While recuperating at Bushnell General Hospital in Brigham City, Utah, Sgt. Stewart was denied physical therapy because of systemic segregation. However, with encouragement from his devoted and optimistic wife, he taught himself to walk with a prosthetic leg by holding on to a pool table in the "colored" hospital medical lounge. This young couple, married less than two years never gave up on their hopes and dreams despite the bitterness, pain, and anger conveyed by "Jim Crow" practices. They persevered through it all.

Richard and Myrtle celebrated 67 years of marriage. Myrtle's gentle giant, Richard, after a long illness, in the care of Myrtle, passed on August 8, 2011, in their home. Myrtle and Richard were reunited in heaven on March 4, 2016, when Myrtle passed after a brief illness, one week after her 99th birthday. A few months later, on a sunny afternoon, the wind rushed through the living room in Marquetta's home. Marquetta and her daughter, Robin, ran to see who had entered. Finding no one, Marquetta and her daughter acknowledged Myrtle's final farewell.

—Marquetta Stewart-Brown, JD & Wilton R. Stewart, PhD

References:

Clark, A. (2020, August 5). Black Americans who served in WWII faced segregation abroad and at home. History. https://www.history.com/news/black-soldiers-world-war-ii-discrimination

Hunter, A. G., & Rollins, A. (2015). We Made History: Collective Memory and the Legacy of the Tuskegee Airmen. Journal of Social Issues, 71(2), 264–278. https://doi.org/10.1111/josi.12109

Marble, S. (Ed.). (2012). Scraping the barrel: The military use of sub-standard manpower. Fordham University Press.

Rostker, B. D. (2013). Providing for the casualties of war: The American experience through World War II. Rand Corporation.

APPENDICES

APPENDIX A: INSPIRATION FOR A GENTLE GIANT

By Myrtle Stewart (edited by Wilton Stewart)

The surprise visit by Sergeant Stewart to Myrtle's home in December of 1943 was initiated by Bessie Arinwine and her husband Roger, who had teased their nephew. Roger Arinwine told his nephew, Richard, that Myrtle Edwards was currently teaching and lived with her sister Irene, but was about to be

Marriage Photograph – July 1, 1944

married. On the contrary, his aunt Bessie said, "*No, she is still available.*" On a bet from Bessie and Roger, Richard went to find out the truth for himself.

Richard's aunt, Bessie Arinwine, was the only person who knew where Myrtle lived and gave her address to Richard. On arriving on that December day at the residence of Myrtle Edwards he discovered she was sick in bed with the flu. After realizing she was sick, Sergeant Stewart left quickly and returned with a large bag of fruit. Myrtle said, "*What does all of this action have to do with me. Why are you here?*" "Well," he says, "*I would like to build you a house.*"

As the conversation continued with Sgt. Stewart standing outside the residence, he asked, "*What are you doing on Christmas day.*" Myrtle replied, "*I am invited to my Aunt Fannie Mae Patton's house for dinner, but my sister Irene may not want me to go outside because of the weather on Christmas day.*" The Sergeant's response, "*I'd like to take you to her home.*" Myrtle said, "*Maybe.*"

On Christmas day Sgt. Richard Stewart rang the doorbell and the door was answered by Myrtle's sister Irene. Irene told Sgt. Stewart that Myrtle was fighting a severe cold. Quickly, Sgt Stewart said, "*Her feet will not have to touch the snowy ground.*" When Myrtle arrived at the front door, Richard picked Myrtle up and placed her in his car and away they went to visit relatives.

From that 1943 Christmas day on, Richard drove 110 miles every weekend in his 1941 two door Chevrolet from Fort Sill,

Oklahoma. By February 1944, they were engaged and the plans for a wedding began. On July 1st, 1944 at about 6:30 in the evening, Richard and Myrtle were joined in matrimony by the Rev. Sylvester Failly in the residence of Bessie and Roger Arinwine on 7th and Stonewall in Oklahoma City. They honey-mooned the following year, in Salt Lake City, Utah. To this union three children were born; Robbie Ann (1946 – passing at birth), Wilton Richard (1947), and Marquetta Rae (1955).

Myrtle, Richard, and family resided in Oklahoma City until 1949, moved west due to the already close relationship of her husband with his maternal aunt Bessie, who had relocated in Los Angeles, California.

Myrtle's first job in Los Angeles was as a seamstress and later floor manager for Candy Jones Garment Shop. Subsequently, in 1956, Myrtle acquired a Civil Service position with the U.S. Postal Service, where she worked for 24 years as a clerk, job instructor, and subsequently as a special distribution clerk before retiring in August 1980.

Richard & Myrtle Stewart

Since May 2004, Myrtle and Richard lived in Chula Vista,

California, with their daughter, Marquetta, son-in-law, Michael, and granddaughter, Robin. She loved writing poetry and phrases of wisdom. This book's namesake poem, A Gentle Giant, was written in May of 2006. In fact, Myrtle was an active member of Toastmasters.[38] She was always prepared to offer an impromptu message and loved being asked to cite a poem or give an inspirational word.

On March 4, 2016, Myrtle left this earth to be with the Lord. She was preceded in death by Richard, her beloved husband of 67 years (August 8, 2011).

---

38 See Appendix G for two speeches written by W. Myrtle Stewart.

APPENDIX B: SISTERS STORY
(An April Fool's Day Story)
By Myrtle Stewart [edited by Wilton Stewart]

Sister Alice, Coila or Cootsy, and Myrt [*are the characters in this story*].

Big sister Alice sees Myrtle near the kitchen.

Alice: "*Myrtle, I cooked a potato pie; come into the kitchen and I will give you a piece of pie to taste. Now, please do not tell Cootsy.*"

As Adults: Myrtle with three of four sisters (Irene not in picture)

A GENTLE GIANT

Myrtle: "*Okay, I will not tell.*"

After a few minutes have gone by and Myrtle has left the kitchen area, Alice approaches Cootsy.

Alice: "*Cootsy, I cooked a potato pie, I am giving you a slice. Now, please do not tell Myrt.*"

Coila: "*Oh, I will not tell.*"

Later that afternoon, Cootsy sees Myrt in the yard and approaches her with a big smile.

Coila: "*Myrt, Alice gave me some potato pie.*"

Alice has intentionally been watching Cootsy interact with Myrt after she left the kitchen. The joke is on Cootsy.

Alice: "*Now, we know who in our family cannot keep a secret.*"

Coila and Myrt turn around and look up at sister Alice with a simple facial expression and body language with their hands that can easily be interpreted. The surprise facial expression of the two girls translates to "Why".

Alice: "*We all say, yes Coila because she was born in April*" (April 21).

APPENDIX C: LITURGICAL DANCE

By Elder Myrtle Stewart

Sound with meditative movements; that is, pondering close and carefully considering the movements to help give emphasis of joyful praise with up-lifted feeling is surely accomplished in Liturgical Dancing. Today beautiful music started piercing the air at Westminster. We notice that a new trend with spirited expression is associated with this beautiful music, and this trend in movement is called "Liturgical Dance". These expressive movements with music can allow an attentive gathering the opportunity to meditate with deep sincerity in prayer and praise for the Lord. In 1 Chronicles 13:8, we learn how David and all the people danced before the Lord with great enthusiasm, accompanied by singing and by instruments. We like to direct our attention to this manner of expressive dancing or pantomiming in order to acknowledge the broad, deep and unlimited ways of praising God. Although we know the fear of erasing antiquity with new changes of expression in praise is always evident.

A GENTLE GIANT

While reviewing 1 Chronicles, chapters 13, 15 and 16, it seems that David danced before the Lord spontaneously. In some of these chapters, however, there seemed to have been some preparation made for his actions in praising the Lord. Is it acceptable to make preparation for Christian services? Yes, but I believe that performers, speakers and others who may be presented to any audience, prepared or not, will undoubtedly be met with some degree of pessimism from more than one critic.

Many people sit still, listen and look while they address their needs to a Greater Power; while they move into divine comfort. How can anyone keep still, or how can anyone miss a heartfelt feeling of joy? It Is amazing how much difference there is in what men see and think. Where one views a hamlet, another a city; where one beholds ugliness, another beauty. Yes, this is an individual privilege, and we can accept this fact without controversy. Sometimes, it is human nature to be so strikingly different that we often find ourselves objecting to the meaningful side of purpose, even when many other people may be receiving joy and happiness. Many people believe that there is more than one kind of religious discourse as a part of a church service...true belief. Why not weave the direction of Christian expression with meditative prompts into the fabric of Christian faith with Liturgical Dancing?

In prayerful praise and imagery...we watch, in awe, the gentle movements of the Liturgical Dancers as they move around with soft tiptoeing spirit, while waving their hands high above their heads and following the flow of music and words with thankfulness and praise. They lift their heads high with their eyes seeming to penetrate the ceiling and gaze into heavens, while words and music peel out the sound, "My God, How Great Thou Art in All the World!"

Can we give these blessed filled moments our prayerful meditation, and carry this imagery of beauty with us daily with smiles? Yes, we can… and every time we feel this spirit moving in our hearts, we can pray even after we depart from our spirit-filled assembly.

APPENDIX D: MOTHER'S PRAYER
By Elder Myrtle Stewart

Lord, at this moment of prayer, thank you for being our Gracious God. And now, let a silence fall on every one for prayers that will touch their friends and loved ones who are in need. — A need for comfort in illness; a need to overcome loneliness, a need to console those that mourn, a need for those wandering in the wilderness that do not know God……Yes, we all need a touch from you Lord.

Help us oh Lord. With a touch by the fruits of the Holy Spirit; love, joy, goodness, kindness, faithfulness, and patience. Let us pray as Jesus prayed with his disciples —

A GENTLE GIANT

"Our Father, which art in heaven,
Hallowed be thy name.
Thy kingdom come.
Thy will be done in earth, as it is in heaven.
Give us this day our daily bread.
And forgive us our debts,
as we forgive our debtors.
And lead us not into temptation, but deliver us from evil:
For thine is the kingdom, and the power, and the glory, forever.
Amen"

(Matt.6:9-13, King James Translation)

APPENDIX E: REFLECTIONS FROM MYRTLE STEWART

1967 – Pepperdine College

By Elder Myrtle Stewart

[This article was first published in the Westminster Presbyterian Church (WPC) Newsletter, Volume 1, Issue 2, January 22, 2009. Several variations of this reflection have been written by Myrtle Stewart. This printing is a compilation of several of those writings.]

I recuperated my poem writing in year 2004 after moving to Chula Vista, Ca. So, time seemed to bring about a different change. I was filled with stress; however, well cared for by our new young family home care givers.

Hobby number one is seamstering and, crafting with remnant materials for odd pillows and other household needs.

Hobby number two has a long story. Since 1967, I have become an enthusiastic memory practitioner. While prayer-fully looking back to the year 1967, when my son, (Capt. Retired, Navy) Wilton R. Stewart was a student at Pepperdine College, he ran home to tell me there is an announcement on our college bulletin board stating that there will be a memory class taught with brilliant demonstrations in memorizing anything that you would like to take into serious consideration. *[The instructor for the class is]* a freelance teacher from Florida University who could not make an acceptable passing score on his law examinations, so he resigned from college attendance.

His disappointment in ability for good memory urged him into action for designing a process for recalling to mind facts previously learned, and past experiences. The young man organized a memory plan that became a freelance miracle for him, as he traveled our country to teach miracles in memory. Although it is a long story, I would like to demonstrate it to interested people someway. I know, let me do it in poem!

APPENDICES

Title: Memory Class Credits

Give memory credits to Wilton Stewart, you should
My visit to memory class was good.

With Freelance Teacher we learned well
He placed forget and memory in adjustment cell.

A primary class seemed too strange,
Yet Freelance Teacher covered a wide range.

We all enjoyed his memory expertise
With special pointing, he aimed to please.

From class we started with thankful hearts,
With one day's training, we were to start.

One day I yelled, where are my keys
With memory practice, I found them with ease.

I like to share these memory thoughts,
So, people can realize the value he taught.

APPENDIX F: CHILDHOOD MEMORIES THAT INSPIRE[39]

Developing Good Habits

Today is mine provided my habits let me possess it.

Habit eventually becomes character; for what you do and repeat becomes you – and your days.

Habits are avenues through which man largely moves,

But not every street leads to where he should go

· · · · · ·

---

39 These words were found among Myrtle's notes and cataloged as inspirational verses for speeches, poems, and articles she would potentially create. The sources of these word passages are unknown; however, some may be considered the original creation of W. Myrtle Stewart.

Enriched by Giving

Giving is better than receiving though it is contrary to popular belief. Of course, receiving is good. If not, giving is not good for you can't have one without the other. A giving is a gathering hand that collects more than it hands out.

※ ※ ※ ※ ※ ※

Money Gets Attention

The love of money is the root of much attention to those who have it.

※ ※ ※ ※ ※ ※

Love Changes the Looks

Nothing gives the world a new look like love.

The oceans are bluer, the grass is greener, the flowers sweeter, the moon brighter.

And, even the old grouch down the street seems nicer.

※ ※ ※ ※ ※ ※

Wisely Silent

When you don't know what to say,
When you don't know how to say it,
When others don't care to hear,
When talking would hurt another,
When you may later regret it,
When quietude is most persuasive,
Remember, the stars shine in silence,
And so, can man.

. . . . . .

Linked to Others

One of man's supreme needs is a link with others. They can hear his sorrow and share his joys. They can steady him when he wobbles. They can lift him when he falls. They can sit beside him when he is sick. They can play with him when he is well.

. . . . . .

(This passage did not have a title)

Friends multiply our joy and divide our grief.

. . . . . .

"Phraseology Help"[40]

1. Be very thankful for every step that you make,
   God has helped the chances you take.

2. Organized phraseology is very good,
   while writing fine advise for your neighborhood.

3. Do not waste time daily while sitting around.

4. Phraseology is good for one each day,
   while giving advice the helpful way.

5. Always try to make your daily moments, healthy,
   wealthy, and wise.

6. Try to make careful daily moments count,
   You may have a need that un-anticipately mount.

7. Good words in advice practice daily,
   Is a wise and wealthy practice.

8. Try to understand people in your neighborhood,

---

40 These phrases that Myrtle Stewart entitled Phraseology Help were found among her notes. It is believed that these numbered phrases were created by her and set aside for potential use at a later date in the construction of poems.

APPENDICES

You may be the one that can help them do good.

9. Phraseology is good work do you see,
   How it can give advice in short verse with a key.

10. Honor those who have earned honor, makes
    _____.

11. All duties carefully done,
    Make our days wonderfully won!

12. Work hard and steady, and do not give up;
    For yourself buy a golden cup.

13. Springtime is flying around,
    I watch them as they decorate your town.

14. Watch your step,
    Or you may end where devil crept.

15. When you have courage, you can get your job on the way,
    So don't give up, make all points display.

APPENDIX G: SPEECHES

The Art of Success
By Madame Toastmaster Myrtle Stewart

In trying to resolve what you ought in life, the answer is in you. The best is up to you. We are neither a born winner nor a born loser. During our early years we were given opportunities to develop and enhance our learning skills by taking daily instructions from our parents, teachers, and leaders. While now, we give attention daily to mechanisms like radio, television, and computers. While these items play a significant part in our educational abilities, there are many avenues in which we are exposed.

We can look back over our past years and say "I failed to use all of my potential." We also have time to speak to ourselves and say may I become wiser, better, and happier. One must begin to realize it is largely internal problems to incorporate trust and confidence and [*overcome*] reluctance [*and doubt*]. Out of the heart are the issues which determine the state of man.

We can resolve to forget past mistakes and press on to higher achievements.

To put first things first. To make our work our joy. To allow nothing to disturb our peace of mind. To never loose self-control. To spend so much time improving ourselves that we have no time for criticism of others. To think the best. Work for it and expect it. To be a friend to man. To stand for right and be true. To be kind. To take every disappointment as a stimulant. To live on the sunny side of every cloud. To smile. To look ahead. To keep moving, remembering that progress is man's distinction. And no matter which way the ball bounces in life it is your game. Play it to win. Yield not to misfortune. Misfortune is real; so is fortune and on the law of averages there should be enough fortune to more than offset misfortune. Chance or misfortune – grab it.

• • • • • •

Impromptu Speech – Homeward[41]

It affords me no little amount of pleasure to be able to worship in the place where I first felt the Holy Spirit and to be able to worship with those whom I was reared and coaxed by.

---

41 Believe this speech was written on a visit to her family church in Longview, Texas after graduation from high school or college. The speech concludes with a poem entitled Somebody's Mother by Mabel Dow Brine (1816-1913).

To talk to you of how I have been using my Sunday time today probably would not be of a very [good] interest to you because you may not believe it. I "shouldn't think," and then you may. But God sees all we do, hear all we say; therefore, it would *[be]* no-body but me if I told you an untruth about it.

But I must pause, and say I am truly grateful to our Pleasant Green elderly leaders and parents in this community. Because I feel very much like you have been praying for your community.

The people with whom I worship seem so much like Pleasant Green community people until I feel like the little boy spoken in a poem once.

[W. Myrtle Stewart read a poem written by Mary Dow Brine (1816-1913) entitled "Somebody's Mother" to conclude her presentation.]